CONTENTS

Section Four — Staging and Design

Section Five — Close Analysis

D1493043

Section Six — Exam Advice

The Characters in 'Blood Brothers'
'Blood Brothers' Cartoon

Published by CGP

Editors:
Emma Cleasby
Heather Cowley
Zoe Fenwick
Sophie Herring
Katya Parkes
Jack Tooth

Contributors:
Sam Milnes
Lucy Thompson
Mike Vogler

With thanks to Holly Robinson, Hannah Roscoe and David Tudor for the proofreading.
With thanks to Emily Smith for the copyright research.

Acknowledgements:

With thanks to David Cooper for permission to use the image on the cover and the images on pages 4, 23, 28, 29, 30, 34, 39, 40, 47, 58, 59, 63 & 65.

With thanks to Alamy for permission to use the images on pages 1, 3, 7, 8, 13 & 38.

With thanks to Photostage for permission to use the images on pages 2, 3, 9, 10, 11, 14, 17, 27, 31, 33, 36, 37, 57, 64, 66, 68 & 69.

With thanks to Kurt Sneddon for permission to use the images on pages 3, 4, 5, 19, 20, 41, 52 & 56 from the Sydney production of Blood Brothers, produced by Enda Markey.

With thanks to Rex Features for permission to use the images on pages 3, 12, 26, 32 & 35.

With thanks to ArenaPAL for permission to use the images on pages 5, 44, 48, 51 & 67.

With thanks to Jeff Busby for permission to use the images on pages 18, 21, 49, 50, 54, 55 & 62 from the Melbourne production of Blood Brothers, produced by Enda Markey.

With thanks to Neil J Halin for permission to use the images on pages 22, 45, 46 & 53.

ISBN: 978 1 78294 966 4
Printed by Elanders Ltd, Newcastle upon Tyne.
Clipart from Corel®

Based on the classic CGP style created by Richard Parsons.

Introduction to 'Blood Brothers'

'Blood Brothers' was written by Willy Russell

1) *Blood Brothers* was written in Britain in the 1980s, but it's set in the period between the 1950s and the 1970s.

2) It's a musical play written by Willy Russell, a British playwright. Russell originally wrote *Blood Brothers* as a straight play, but he later adapted it into a musical, adding songs and lyrics.

3) *Blood Brothers* includes elements of tragedy — it has serious themes, an unhappy ending and one of its main characters experiences a downfall.

4) However, there are also light-hearted and humorous moments that provide comic relief for the audience.

Take a look at p.12 for more on Willy Russell and his plays.

Blood Brothers on Stage

Directors need to think about the key features of *Blood Brothers* before they produce it on stage. Aspects like the play's 20th-century setting might influence how it is performed and designed.

It's a play about social class and identity

Blood Brothers tells the story of twin brothers who were separated at birth and grew up in different social classes. The play's themes focus on how a person's life can be influenced by things beyond their control.

1) **Social Class** — The play shows that the class you are born into influences how you are treated and the opportunities you have.

2) **Identity** — Russell questions whether a person's upbringing or their nature (genetic make-up) is more important in deciding their identity and the path their life follows.

3) **Gender** — The story highlights the impact of society's expectations about gender on the lives of men and women.

4) **Childhood and Growing Up** — Childhood is portrayed as easy and carefree, but life is shown to be more difficult in adulthood.

5) **Fate** — Russell explores the idea that people's lives are controlled by fate, and that they're unable to escape it.

Directors should consider the themes that they want to emphasise when making their production decisions. For example, the Narrator might remain on stage at all times and watch over the other characters to reinforce that the twins can't avoid their fate.

The play reflected British society at the time

1) The play's characters are fictional, but Russell uses them to comment on real social issues that existed in British society in the 1980s when the play was first performed:

- There was a strong class divide in 1980s Britain. Middle-class people had more opportunities than working-class people. This was reflected in things like education, job prospects and wealth.
- Britain also had a serious unemployment problem in the 1980s. Many working-class people like Mickey lost their jobs when the government closed traditional industries (see p.6).

© Trinity Mirror / Mirrorpix / Alamy Stock Photo

2) Russell aims to show that the differences caused by social class are unfair and that these inequalities created many of the social problems that existed in 1980s Britain. This message challenges the view held by the government at the time (see p.6), which claimed that anyone could be successful as long as they worked hard.

By exploring issues that were familiar to his audience, Russell encourages people to apply the message of the play to their own lives.

Introduction to 'Blood Brothers'

'Blood Brothers' still appeals to audiences today

1) Although *Blood Brothers* is set over 40 years ago, many of the issues it explores are still relevant today:

- Russell's message that social class can be restrictive applies today — class division is now less rigid, but class continues to influence the opportunities that are available to people.
- The play explores social issues that exist in today's society. For example, unemployment is still a problem, and many people still face prejudice because of their gender.
- Some of the themes in the play are universal — *Blood Brothers* explores ideas about identity and the inevitable nature of fate that are recognisable in any era.

Effect on the Audience

Blood Brothers deals with issues that are recognisable to the audience, so it's easier for them to relate to the characters and sympathise with them. This helps the audience to engage with the play's message.

2) The dramatic features of *Blood Brothers* make it entertaining. The storyline is dark and tragic, but there are also moments of comedy — this makes the play exciting to watch, as the audience don't know what might happen next.

3) The plot is fast paced, which keeps the audience engaged — the events of more than twenty years are played out on stage in the space of two acts.

4) The play's songs are entertaining and emotional. They bring the story to life for the audience and make watching the play a more memorable experience.

See Section Two for more on the play's dramatic features and the techniques that Russell uses.

'Blood Brothers' has been performed many times

1) The musical version of *Blood Brothers* was first performed in 1983 at the Liverpool Playhouse.

2) It was immediately popular in Liverpool and was soon transferred to the Lyric Theatre in London's West End.

3) *Blood Brothers* has been performed all over the UK — there have been several national tours of the play since it opened.

4) After its initial run in 1983, *Blood Brothers* went on to become one of the longest-running musicals ever performed in the West End — it ran continuously from 1988 until 2012.

5) The play is still popular today — a special anniversary tour of *Blood Brothers* opened in 2017 and was extended for 2018.

© Donald Cooper/ photostage

The Johnstones sing 'Bright New Day' in the original West End production of the play in London in 1983.

Blood Brothers has also had international success

- The play has been performed in several countries including Australia, Japan, Canada and the USA — its universal themes make it appealing to audiences all over the world.
- It's even been translated into another language. In 1993, the play was performed in Czech-Slovak in Slovakia.
- In 2013, an adaptation of the play was performed in South Africa. The original play was altered to reflect issues that were relevant to South African society.

You won't need to write about adaptations in your exam, but it's useful to see how directors have presented the play in different ways depending on the identity and experiences of their audience.

Who's Who in 'Blood Brothers'

Mrs Johnstone...

... is Mickey, Edward and Sammy's mother. She gives Edward up so he'll have a better life.

Mrs Lyons...

... is a middle-class woman who longs for a child. She manipulates Mrs Johnstone into giving Edward to her.

Mickey Johnstone...

... is the twin Mrs Johnstone keeps. He's a friendly child but ends up unemployed and in trouble with the law.

Edward Lyons...

... is the twin Mrs Lyons takes. He's well-educated and grows up to be a successful local councillor.

Linda...

... is Mickey and Edward's friend. Both boys fall in love with her, and she marries Mickey.

Sammy Johnstone...

... is Mickey's older brother. He's always in trouble as a child and ends up as a criminal.

Mr Lyons...

... is a wealthy businessman who spends more time at work than with his family.

Chorus Members...

... sing parts of the story and play some minor characters, such as the 'Dole-ites'.

The Narrator...

... helps to tell the story. He also plays several minor characters throughout the play.

Introduction

Plot Summary

© David Cooper Photo

'Blood Brothers'... what happens when?

Here's a little recap of the main events of *Blood Brothers*. It's a good idea to learn what happens when, so you can consider how elements of performance and design might change as the plot progresses.

Act One — The twins are born and separated

- The Narrator introduces the twins and gives an <u>overview</u> of the story. We see a <u>preview</u> of the play's final moments — Mickey and Edward <u>both die</u>.

- Mrs Johnstone sings about how her husband left her with <u>seven children</u> and she <u>can't afford</u> to feed them.

© David Cooper Photo

- Mrs Johnstone goes to clean at Mrs Lyons's house. Mrs Lyons reveals that she and her husband <u>can't have children</u>.

- Mrs Johnstone finds out she is <u>pregnant</u> with twins. Mrs Lyons <u>persuades</u> her to give her one of the babies.

- Mrs Johnstone gives birth. Debt collectors <u>repossess</u> her belongings. Mrs Lyons <u>takes</u> one of the babies.

- Mrs Lyons <u>fires</u> Mrs Johnstone, and tells her that both boys will <u>die</u> if they ever find out they are twins.

Act One — The boys meet, aged seven, and are separated again

- Mickey and Edward <u>meet</u> near Mickey's house. They <u>bond immediately</u>.

- Mrs Johnstone is <u>horrified</u> when she realises who Mickey's new friend is. She tells Edward to <u>leave</u> and not to come back.

- Mickey goes to see Edward but Mrs Lyons sends him away. Edward is <u>angry</u> and uses <u>swear words</u> he learnt from Mickey. Mrs Lyons <u>hits</u> him.

- Edward <u>sneaks out</u> to play with Mickey and Linda.

- Mrs Lyons tells her husband that they need to <u>move away</u>, but he's <u>unconvinced</u>. Soon afterwards, a policeman catches Mickey, Edward and Linda <u>misbehaving</u>, which persuades Mr Lyons to move his family.

© Australian Production 2015 / Produced by Enda Markey / Photograph by Kurt Sneddon

- Edward goes to Mrs Johnstone's house <u>upset</u> about moving. She gives him a <u>locket</u> with a picture of her and Mickey in it.

- The Johnstones find out that they're being moved to <u>Skelmersdale</u>.

Introduction

Plot Summary

Act Two — The boys meet again as teenagers

- The Johnstones are <u>happier</u> in Skelmersdale.

- Edward is <u>suspended</u> from his boarding school.
  Mickey and Linda are <u>suspended</u> from
  their comprehensive school.

- Back home, Mickey and Edward meet and <u>recognise</u>
  each other. They <u>renew</u> their friendship.

- Mrs Lyons sees the boys together. She tries to <u>bribe</u>
  Mrs Johnstone to <u>move away</u>. When she refuses,
  Mrs Lyons tries to <u>attack</u> her with a knife.

© Elliott Franks / ArenaPAL

- Mickey, Edward and Linda <u>meet up</u> and the play moves through scenes in which they age from <u>14 to 18</u>.

- Edward reveals he <u>loves</u> Linda, but then <u>encourages Mickey</u> to ask her out. Edward <u>leaves</u> for university.

- Mickey and Linda get married because Linda is <u>pregnant</u>. Mickey loses his job and has to
  go on the <u>dole</u>. Edward comes home from university. Mickey <u>resents</u> him and they <u>fall out</u>.

- Edward <u>proposes</u> to Linda. She <u>admits</u> she has feelings for him, but tells him she's married to Mickey.

- Sammy <u>persuades</u> Mickey to be a lookout during a robbery. It goes <u>wrong</u> and Sammy <u>shoots</u> the petrol
  station attendant. Mickey is sentenced to <u>seven years</u> in jail. He becomes <u>depressed</u> and is put on <u>pills</u>.

Act Two — The boys are now adults

- Mickey is released <u>early</u> but he is still depressed. Linda begs him to <u>stop</u> taking the pills.

- Linda gets them a <u>new house</u> and finds a <u>job</u> for Mickey. Mickey knows
  that Edward, who is now a <u>local councillor</u>, is responsible for both.

© Australian Production 2015 / Produced by
Enda Markey / Photograph by Kurt Sneddon

- Linda and Edward <u>kiss</u>. Meanwhile,
  Mickey <u>stops</u> taking his pills.

- <u>Mrs Lyons</u> shows Mickey that
  Edward and Linda are <u>together</u>.

- Mickey takes the <u>gun</u> Sammy used in the
  robbery and <u>confronts</u> Edward at the Town Hall.

- Mrs Johnstone tells the boys they are <u>brothers</u>.
  Mickey loses control and accidentally <u>shoots</u>
  <u>Edward</u>. The police <u>shoot Mickey</u> in response.

And you thought your family drama was bad...

So... directors producing *Blood Brothers* have loads to consider. There's tragedy, comedy, more time jumps than you can shake a stick at and loads of social messages (not to mention all that singing and dancing). With so much going on, it's important you know the plot really well. Check out the cartoon at the back of this book if you're still not sure.

Britain in the Late 20th Century

The late 20th century was a different world — mobile phones were enormous, the Internet was barely a thing and you weren't allowed to leave the house without wearing denim. At least that's what my brother told me...

The play is set in Britain between the 1950s and 1970s

1) Russell doesn't say exactly <u>when</u> the play is set, but characters make references to some <u>real-life issues</u> of the late <u>1960s</u> and early <u>1970s</u> — Mr Lyons talks about the "shrinking pound" and the rising "price of oil".

2) These issues were consequences of an <u>economic recession</u> that Britain experienced during this period — the economy went into <u>decline</u> and people were <u>earning</u> and <u>spending</u> less money.

3) Traditional industries like <u>shipbuilding</u> and <u>coal mining</u> were <u>badly affected</u>. These industries often employed <u>whole communities</u> of <u>working-class men</u> who relied on these jobs for their <u>livelihood</u>.

4) Margaret Thatcher became Prime Minister in 1979. She <u>closed down</u> lots of <u>traditional industries</u> because she thought they <u>weren't profitable</u>. This meant lots of people <u>lost their jobs</u>, particularly in <u>working-class</u> communities.

Staging and Design

Designers might use the play's <u>context</u> to make its <u>settings</u> seem more <u>authentic</u>. They could use <u>fashions</u> from the 1950s, 1960s and 1970s in their <u>costume</u> and <u>set</u> designs to make them more <u>believable</u>.

The action takes place in Liverpool and Skelmersdale

Act One is set in Liverpool and Act Two is set in Skelmersdale — a town that's located to the <u>northeast</u> of the city. Here are the <u>key locations</u> in the play:

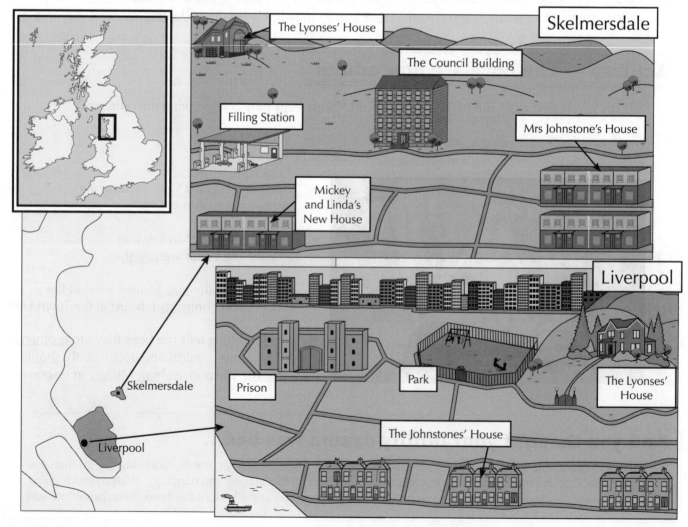

Britain in the Late 20th Century

Living conditions varied in Liverpool in the 1960s

Some working-class people in Liverpool lived in dilapidated slums after the Second World War.

1) Like the Johnstones, many <u>working-class</u> people in Liverpool lived in <u>council houses</u> — these were owned by the city council and rented to tenants.

2) Many of these council houses were <u>small</u> and <u>overcrowded</u>. Most had no <u>heating</u>, <u>indoor toilets</u> or <u>gardens</u>. They were often <u>constructed</u> from <u>cheap materials</u> like concrete — they had been built <u>quickly</u> after the Second World War to replace housing lost during <u>bombing raids</u>.

3) However, Liverpool also had <u>affluent areas</u> where <u>middle-class people</u> lived — housing in these areas was <u>larger</u> and <u>better quality</u>, and there was more <u>open space</u> than in <u>crowded</u> working-class areas. In the play, the Lyonses' house is located "up in the <u>park</u>" and is described as "<u>lovely</u>" and "<u>large</u>".

A <u>set designer</u> might emphasise the <u>different living conditions</u> that the Johnstones and the Lyonses experience (see p.46). This would reinforce the play's <u>message</u> about the impact of <u>social class</u> on <u>everyday life</u>.

The council moved people to Skelmersdale

1) In the 1960s, the city council in Liverpool tried to <u>relieve</u> the city's <u>overcrowding</u> problem. They moved some of their tenants from <u>Liverpool</u> to <u>Skelmersdale</u> — a <u>New Town</u> in the <u>countryside</u>. This town was already home to many <u>middle-class</u> people.

2) Some residents were <u>happy</u> about being <u>moved</u> — in the play, Mrs Johnstone is <u>excited</u> when she is moved to Skelmersdale because she thinks that <u>living conditions</u> will be <u>better</u> there. Other residents felt that <u>communities</u> were being <u>broken up</u>, and they were <u>reluctant</u> to leave the areas they'd grown up in.

New Towns

Overcrowding was a <u>serious problem</u> in Britain's cities after the Second World War, so the <u>government</u> created <u>New Towns</u> — these were <u>existing towns</u> that were <u>redeveloped</u> to provide <u>more housing</u> for nearby cities.

Housing conditions were much better in Skelmersdale

1) New Towns like Skelmersdale were full of <u>newly built</u> housing — homes <u>weren't falling apart</u> like many of the council houses in Liverpool, and they were <u>cleaner</u>, <u>safer</u> and more <u>modern</u>.

2) These towns were also <u>well planned</u> — there was more <u>open space</u> than in the city, and properties were often <u>larger</u>. In the play, Mrs Johnstone is excited to have a <u>garden</u> in her new house.

Social Class

- There was still a <u>division</u> between <u>working-class</u> and <u>middle-class</u> people in New Towns. The <u>new housing</u> that the government built for <u>working-class residents</u> from the city was often <u>grouped together</u> in large <u>council estates</u> that were attached to the existing town.

- This <u>separation</u> is reflected in the play — Mickey lives on "The <u>estate</u>", while Edward lives in "that <u>big house</u> on the <u>hill</u>", which suggests that he lives in part of the <u>original town</u>.

You know what they say — New Town, new me...

It's important that you understand the social and historical context of the play. In the exam, you'll need to be able to link the play's context to the design choices that you'd make when staging *Blood Brothers*.

Social Class

Social class is a really big theme in the play. Huge. Massive. Gigantic. If you're not thinking about social class when you're working on *Blood Brothers*, then we're probably not talking about the same play...

Working-class people had fewer opportunities

1) In *Blood Brothers*, Russell shows that a person's social class can determine the course of their life. He uses Mickey and Edward to demonstrate this to the audience — Edward's middle-class upbringing gives him many opportunities that Mickey doesn't get from his working-class background.

	Britain in the late 20th century	*Blood Brothers*
Middle Class	• Middle-class people often received a better education than working-class people. They could afford to live in areas with good schools, and some sent their children to private schools. • This gave them access to university and well-paid jobs that provided financial security.	• Edward goes to a private boarding school, and he's expected to attend "Oxbridge" (this refers to two prestigious British universities — Oxford and Cambridge). • Despite being suspended, he does very well at school and goes to university. This allows him to get a high-status job as a councillor when he leaves education.
Working Class	• Working-class people often couldn't afford to go to university — they had to get a job so they could earn money and support their family instead. • As a result, many were stuck in low-paid jobs for the rest of their working lives.	• Mickey goes to a state school and he is expected to get a job as soon as he leaves school, instead of going to university. • He gets a menial job, which he then loses, and he isn't qualified to do anything else.

2) When Mickey finds out that Edward is his twin brother, he shouts "I could have been him!" This emphasises the important role that class and background have played in shaping the twins' lives.

> **Identity**
>
> Russell suggests that nurture (upbringing) is more important than nature (genetics) when it comes to a person's identity and the path their life follows.

The recession had a bigger impact on the working class

1) In the 1970s, there was widespread unemployment among the working class because of the recession, and many people had to live off state benefits (money paid to them by the government). They struggled to afford basic things like food and clothes. This led to an increase in depression and crime rates.

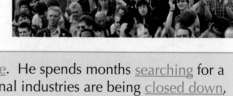

© Homer Sykes Archive / Alamy Stock Photo

2) In contrast, middle-class people were mostly unaffected by the unemployment crisis — they didn't rely on traditional industries for employment and had a wider variety of jobs available to them.

3) This contrast is reflected in Act Two of the play:

- Mickey loses his low-paid job and is forced to go on the dole. He spends months searching for a new job, but can't find anything — the factories and traditional industries are being closed down, and he doesn't have the qualifications to do anything else. He eventually turns to crime.
- The middle-class Lyonses aren't affected in the same way as the working-class characters. Mr Lyons fires his employees at the factory, but he keeps his job. His family stays wealthy — Edward stays at university and doesn't need to work. He tells Mickey "I've got money, plenty of it".

Social Class

Class was associated with behaviour in the 1960s and 1970s

1) In the late 20th century, there were <u>stereotypes</u> about the way that people from certain social classes <u>behaved</u>. The <u>attitudes</u> of some characters in the play <u>reflect</u> these ideas:

   - Mrs Johnstone thinks <u>middle-class</u> children are <u>polite</u> and <u>well behaved</u> — she says that her child wouldn't <u>fight</u> or <u>swear</u> if he were raised by Mrs Lyons.
   - Mrs Lyons thinks that <u>working-class</u> children are <u>badly behaved</u> — she worries that Edward will behave "like a <u>horrible</u> little boy, like <u>them</u>" if he keeps seeing Mickey.

2) When the twins meet in Act One, they seem to <u>fulfil</u> these expectations — Edward has <u>good manners</u>, while Mickey teaches Edward how to <u>swear</u>.

3) The play reflects stereotypes about <u>class</u> and <u>appearance</u> too — Mickey notices that Edward is "<u>clean</u>, <u>neat</u> and <u>tidy</u>" while Edward mentions Mickey being "<u>untidy</u>".

4) <u>Class stereotypes</u> affected the way that people from different social classes were <u>treated</u> by <u>society</u>. For example, when Mickey and Edward get in trouble in Act One, the <u>Policeman</u> considers Mickey's actions to be more <u>serious</u> — the Policeman's <u>class prejudice</u> (see p.40) means that he associates <u>criminal behaviour</u> with the <u>working class</u>.

> **Effect on the Audience**
>
> Many characters in the play are presented as <u>class stereotypes</u>, which makes their class background <u>recognisable</u> to the audience. This means Russell can use these characters to convey <u>messages</u> about working-class and middle-class people in <u>general</u>.

Money gives some characters power

1) <u>Money</u> was one of the <u>factors</u> that determined which <u>class</u> a person belonged to in the late 20th century — middle-class people were <u>far wealthier</u> than working-class people.

2) In *Blood Brothers*, <u>wealth</u> is associated with <u>power</u>. For example, Mrs Lyons is able to use <u>money</u> to try to <u>solve</u> her <u>problems</u>:

   - In Act One, she uses her husband's money to <u>bribe</u> Mrs Johnstone to <u>stay away</u> from Edward. Mrs Lyons "<u>pushes</u>" money into Mrs Johnstone's hands — this highlights the <u>link</u> between <u>class</u>, <u>money</u> and <u>power</u>.
   - When Mrs Lyons wants to <u>move</u> to Skelmersdale to get away from the Johnstones, the Lyonses are able to buy a <u>new house</u> almost immediately.

The Narrator warns Mrs Johnstone about the consequences of giving Edward away. The bank notes highlight the role that money has played in her decision.

© Donald Cooper/ photostage

3) In contrast, the <u>working-class</u> characters don't have this <u>power</u> — their <u>lack</u> of money <u>forces</u> them into <u>difficult situations</u>. Mrs Johnstone <u>can't afford</u> to keep both twins so she gives one away, and Mickey turns to <u>crime</u> when he can't find a job.

> **Effect on the Audience**
>
> This contrast conveys the <u>message</u> that <u>middle-class people</u> have more <u>control</u> over their lives than <u>working-class people</u> as a result of their <u>wealth</u>.

Everyone loves 'Blood Brothers' — it's a real class act...

Social class affects everything — and I mean everything — in *Blood Brothers*. Consider how you could use performance and design to convey Russell's message about the impact of class division in society.

Family Structure and Gender

Even though they get a shout-out in the title, *Blood Brothers* isn't just about Mickey and Edward — Russell's interested in motherhood and family, and he uses his characters to explore these themes throughout the play.

Family structure was often traditional in the 1960s

© Donald Cooper/ photostage

1) There was major <u>social change</u> in the 1960s. For example, <u>homosexuality</u> was decriminalised in 1967, and <u>divorce</u> was made easier in 1969.

2) However, many people's <u>attitudes</u> remained <u>traditional</u>. Families were expected to have a '<u>nuclear</u>' structure — where a family is made up of a <u>mother</u>, a <u>father</u> and their <u>children</u>.

3) There were certain <u>gender roles</u> that men and women were expected to <u>fulfil</u> in these traditional nuclear families — the <u>man</u> went to <u>work</u> and earned <u>money</u> for his family, while the <u>woman</u> looked after the <u>house</u> and <u>children</u>.

4) Russell uses <u>stereotypes</u> of different family structures in the play:

> • The Johnstones are an example of a <u>single-parent family</u>, where Mrs Johnstone has to fulfil the traditional roles of <u>both parents</u>. In the 1960s, <u>single-parent families</u> like the Johnstones were <u>less common</u> and often <u>frowned upon</u>.
>
> • The Lyonses are presented as a <u>typical nuclear family</u>, but they're <u>not happy</u>. Russell shows that the '<u>ideal</u>' family structure doesn't always lead to a <u>happy</u> and <u>stable</u> life.

Effect on the Audience

Today, audiences are <u>used</u> to seeing a <u>wide variety</u> of <u>family structures</u>, so they might receive the play <u>differently</u> than <u>audiences</u> did in the late 20th century.

5) These <u>social issues</u> would have been <u>relevant</u> to audiences in the <u>1980s</u> — <u>single-parent families</u> were becoming more common, <u>divorce rates</u> were rising and <u>gender roles</u> were starting to <u>change</u>.

Russell explores the impact of social expectations about gender

1) The play shows that <u>gender roles</u> are <u>restrictive</u> for women. For example, Mrs Lyons often can't make <u>decisions</u> without her <u>husband's approval</u>. The couple remain <u>childless</u> because Mr Lyons is <u>unwilling</u> to <u>adopt</u>, and she has to <u>ask</u> her husband for <u>money</u> when she wants to buy things.

Social Class and Gender

Russell shows that while Mrs Lyons has <u>power</u> due to her <u>social class</u>, she's still <u>limited</u> by her <u>gender</u>.

2) Linda's <u>character arc</u> illustrates how <u>difficult</u> it is to <u>escape</u> gender roles — as a <u>child</u>, she <u>defies gender roles</u> and does everything the boys do, but as a <u>woman</u> she is <u>trapped</u> in a life where she's "<u>washed</u> a million <u>dishes</u>" and is "always <u>making tea</u>".

3) The play shows that trying to <u>fulfil</u> gender expectations can cause <u>suffering</u>:

> • Mrs Lyons feels she has <u>failed</u> as a <u>woman</u> because she doesn't have <u>children</u>. She is <u>desperate</u> to have a <u>child</u> and this <u>motivates</u> her actions in the play.
>
> • In the play, <u>men</u> are also <u>negatively affected</u> by gender roles — as a man, Mickey is expected to <u>provide</u> for his family, and he feels <u>worthless</u> when he <u>loses his job</u> and isn't able to <u>support</u> Linda and their daughter.

Gender — it can be the role of a lifetime...

You should be prepared to write about the social context of the play in the exam — think about how the gender expectations of the time might influence the way that the characters interact with one another.

Growing Up in Late 20th-Century Britain

The play follows the twins from tiny babies to stroppy teens to troubled adults. Oh, they grow up so fast...

Childhood is presented as a time of innocence

1) As children, the brothers are <u>carefree</u> — they run around <u>playing games</u> and getting into <u>mischief</u>. They imitate the violent behaviour of "<u>cowboys and Indians</u>" and <u>gangsters</u> from popular <u>American movies</u> of the day, but there are <u>no lasting consequences</u> because "The whole thing's just a <u>game</u>".

2) Russell shows that friendship is <u>easy</u> for the twins as <u>children</u>. Edward asks Mickey to be his "<u>best friend</u>" when they first meet, and Mickey <u>accepts</u> his offer right away.

3) It <u>doesn't matter</u> to the twins that they're from <u>different backgrounds</u> — when Sammy calls Edward "<u>a friggin' poshy</u>", Mickey says "<u>No, he's not</u>. He's my best friend." The boys <u>realise</u> that they live different lives, but they <u>don't understand</u> that this is because of their <u>social class</u>.

'Youth culture' was on the rise in the 1960s

1) By the 1960s, '<u>teenagers</u>' were recognised as a <u>separate group</u> from children and adults, with different <u>interests</u> and <u>behaviours</u>. They used <u>fashion</u>, <u>music</u> and <u>hobbies</u> to express themselves.

2) Youth culture was associated with being <u>free</u> and <u>rebellious</u>. Russell uses Mickey, Linda and Edward's <u>teenage years</u> to reflect this.

3) Act Two shows Mickey, Edward and Linda at the <u>rifle range</u> and the <u>beach</u> — this highlights the <u>happy lives</u> they have as <u>teenagers</u> before they become <u>adults</u> and struggle with their <u>responsibilities</u>.

> **Effect on the Audience**
>
> This heightens the <u>tragedy</u> of the play — Mickey, Edward and Linda's lives seem to be <u>full of promise</u>, but the audience knows that the twins are going to <u>die</u>.

Friendships change as the characters get older

1) As <u>young adults</u>, the twins' <u>different lifestyles</u> push them <u>apart</u>. Mickey has to take on <u>adult responsibilities</u> — he gets a <u>job</u> and becomes a <u>father</u>. Edward goes to <u>university</u> and doesn't have the same <u>responsibilities</u> — he's "still a <u>kid</u>" compared to Mickey.

2) They also become <u>aware</u> of <u>class prejudices</u> and how they are <u>separated</u> by the <u>class divide</u>. Mickey <u>resents</u> that Edward has a much <u>easier life</u>, and Edward <u>doesn't understand</u> why money is such a <u>worry</u> for Mickey.

3) As the twins grow up, the <u>power</u> in their relationship <u>shifts</u>. Mickey holds the power as a <u>child</u> — Edward <u>aspires</u> to be like Mickey, and is influenced by him. As <u>adults</u>, Edward holds the power. His <u>money</u> and <u>influence</u> mean that he is able to <u>provide</u> for Mickey when Mickey loses his job.

© Donald Cooper/ photostage

Both Mickey and Edward develop feelings for Linda as they grow up. This adds to the strain on their friendship.

REVISION TASK

It's all fun and games until you leave secondary school...

Imagine you're Mickey when he gets married and is fired from his job at the factory in Act Two. Write a paragraph explaining your feelings. You should think about the following points:

1) How you feel about the new pressures in your life.
2) What you think will happen to your relationship with Linda.

> Putting yourself in the same situation as the characters in the play could give you ideas on how to direct or perform these characters.

Willy Russell

Plays with songs, without songs and plays that would later have songs — Russell's done it all. His upbringing has greatly influenced his works, as they explore social class (a lot) and are a tad obsessed with Liverpool.

Willy Russell is a British playwright

1) Russell was born in <u>1947</u> to a <u>working-class</u> family and grew up near <u>Liverpool</u>.

2) *Blood Brothers* is one of several <u>famous plays</u> written by Russell. One of his earliest plays also had music in it — *John, Paul, George, Ringo ... and Bert* was about <u>The Beatles</u> (who also came from Liverpool) and featured the band's <u>songs</u>. He was already <u>known</u> for *Educating Rita* when he wrote *Blood Brothers*, and he went on to write other <u>successful</u> plays.

3) Russell's <u>upbringing</u> has <u>influenced</u> his <u>writing</u>. His plays are often set in <u>Liverpool</u> and focus on the <u>struggles</u> of <u>working-class</u> characters.

© Maggie Hardie/REX/Shutterstock

4) His <u>style</u> is influenced by the early 20th-century German playwright and director, <u>Bertolt Brecht</u>:

- Brecht believed that <u>theatre</u> should explore <u>political ideas</u>. He thought that plays should make the audience <u>think</u> and even <u>change</u> their <u>attitudes</u>, rather than just <u>entertain</u>. He is associated with <u>epic theatre</u>, a style of theatre which uses <u>non-naturalistic</u> elements to remind the audience that they are <u>watching a play</u>. This encourages the audience to <u>focus</u> on the <u>message</u> of the play.

- *Blood Brothers* includes <u>non-naturalistic</u> features. For example, Russell recommends using "*the <u>minimum</u> of properties and furniture*" in productions of the play — this provides fewer visual <u>distractions</u>, which allows the audience to <u>concentrate</u> on the play's <u>message</u>.

5) Russell was also influenced by the <u>social</u> and <u>political</u> context of the <u>1980s</u>. The economic recession made <u>class division</u> worse, and many playwrights were writing about <u>class</u> and <u>inequality</u> at this time.

His plays have a strong social message

1) Russell's plays often explore <u>social inequality</u> and the <u>problems</u> faced by <u>working-class</u> people.

2) His protagonists are often <u>working-class women</u>, like Mrs Johnstone, who want to <u>escape</u> their <u>ordinary lives</u>. Russell uses these characters to <u>comment</u> on wider <u>social issues</u>, such as <u>class</u> and <u>gender</u>.

3) His plays often demonstrate how the <u>class system</u> can <u>hold back</u> working-class people through <u>prejudice</u> and <u>lack of opportunities</u>. In *Blood Brothers*, Mickey and Edward live very <u>different lives</u> just because of the <u>class</u> they grew up in (see p.8).

4) Russell wants his audiences to think about the <u>impact</u> of <u>class division</u>. At the <u>end</u> of *Blood Brothers*, the Narrator asks whether "superstition" or "class" is <u>responsible</u> for the twins' deaths. This encourages the <u>audience</u> to reflect on who is to <u>blame</u> for the issues facing the working-class.

Effect on the Audience

Blood Brothers was originally written to be performed in <u>schools</u> (see p.14). Russell wanted to teach <u>children</u> about the role of <u>social class</u> in Britain and the <u>unfairness</u> that was created by class division.

REVISION TASK

Here's a revision task I Russelled up earlier...

Imagine you're directing a production of 'Blood Brothers'. Write a paragraph explaining how you would emphasise Russell's message that class differences create unfairness. Think about:

1) Examples of social inequality that exist in the play.

2) How you would highlight these inequalities for the audience when staging the play.

It's important to think about Russell's intentions when making decisions about performance and design.

The Play on Stage

Now for some lovely pages on theatre conventions and past productions. You'll thank me for this later.

British theatre was changing in the late 20th century

1) Before the 1950s, <u>theatre</u> was often considered to be a <u>middle-class</u> activity — many plays were written to <u>appeal</u> to middle-class <u>audiences</u> and most <u>actors</u> were from a middle-class <u>background</u>.

2) In the 1970s, an <u>alternative theatre</u> movement was developed by smaller companies who <u>rejected</u> the <u>traditions</u> of British theatre. They were more <u>daring</u> and <u>experimental</u>. For example, they used <u>improvisation</u> to create a play or performed in <u>public spaces</u> rather than formal theatres.

3) More <u>regional theatres</u> were built in the 1970s, which made theatre <u>accessible</u> to more people across the country. Playwrights began to <u>embrace</u> subjects that were relevant to <u>regional</u> communities, and plays featured more <u>working-class characters</u>.

4) From the 1960s, more <u>children</u> were introduced to drama through the <u>Theatre in Education</u> movement, where theatre companies performed plays in <u>schools</u>. The plays usually had a <u>strong message</u> and <u>educational purpose</u>. Russell wrote *Blood Brothers* for a Theatre in Education company (see p.14).

5) Many playwrights were influenced by the <u>social issues</u> and <u>politics</u> of the time. Some were <u>critical</u> of <u>Thatcher's government</u> — for example, Jim Cartwright's *Road* shows the results of <u>unemployment</u> on a <u>working-class</u> community in Lancashire.

> See p.6 for more on Thatcher's government.

End of Censorship

British theatre had traditionally been quite <u>conservative</u> — since the 18th century, all plays had to be <u>approved</u> before they could be performed. The <u>Theatres Act</u> of 1968 <u>ended</u> this <u>censorship</u> and plays began to include more <u>controversial</u> themes and <u>shocking</u> content (e.g. <u>graphic violence</u>).

Musicals became more popular in the 1980s

1) Funding cuts in the 1970s and 1980s meant that theatre was often sponsored by <u>private companies</u> who wanted to make <u>money</u>. They backed the <u>most profitable</u> plays — <u>large-scale</u> productions that were suited to <u>long runs</u> and could be reproduced <u>worldwide</u>.

2) This led to the rise of the '<u>megamusical</u>' — <u>large-scale</u> shows featuring <u>special effects</u> and very little <u>spoken dialogue</u>. *Blood Brothers* can be described as a <u>megamusical</u>, but it <u>doesn't fit</u> all of the criteria — for example, it contains a lot of <u>spoken dialogue</u> as well as singing.

3) Other <u>genres</u> and <u>styles</u>, such as <u>pantomime-style</u> performances, <u>comedies</u> and <u>dramas</u>, were <u>popular</u> in British theatre at this time too.

British theatre became known for extravagant shows such as 'Cats' that were produced on a grand scale.

There wasn't a specific set of theatre conventions in the 1980s

1) The <u>theatre conventions</u> of a certain period are the features of the style of <u>staging</u>, <u>design</u> and <u>performance</u> that were in use at that <u>time</u>. By the <u>1980s</u>, a <u>wide variety</u> of different <u>styles</u> and <u>conventions</u> had developed and were being used in British theatre.

2) This meant that Russell <u>didn't have</u> a clear set of conventions to follow — he <u>chose</u> to use a <u>mixture</u> of naturalistic and non-naturalistic conventions in *Blood Brothers* (see p.19).

> <u>Directors</u> can <u>choose</u> whether or not to <u>follow</u> Russell's <u>conventions</u> in their productions. However, they should still consider the <u>effects</u> that Russell might have intended to create and take these into account when making <u>decisions</u> about <u>performance</u> and <u>design</u>.

The Play on Stage

The play was very well received

1) Russell originally wrote *Blood Brothers* for the Merseyside Young People's Theatre Company — this Theatre in Education project performed plays in schools around Liverpool. This version of the play only included one song.

2) Russell began adapting the play into a musical straight away, and this musical version of *Blood Brothers* was first performed at the Liverpool Playhouse in 1983.

3) The play was an immediate success with critics and audiences. After the initial run in Liverpool, it was moved to London's West End, where it won the Olivier Award for Best New Musical. This was followed by a national tour, and the play's popularity continued.

4) Russell made changes to the play before it opened in the West End — he rewrote and restructured parts of Act Two while it was still showing in Liverpool, and then added the rewrites during rehearsals in London.

Barbara Dickson as Mrs Johnstone in 1983.

© Donald Cooper/ photostage

5) Russell worked with fellow Liverpudlian Bill Kenwright to produce another national tour in 1988. Kenwright took the play back to the West End later that year, where it ran for 24 years until 2012 — in 2018, it was the third longest-running musical ever performed in the West End.

6) While *Blood Brothers* was a popular musical that was suited to commercial success, it also had an important social message, as many dramas did in the 1970s and 1980s.

'Blood Brothers' has been staged in different ways

1) In the original 1983 production of the play, the set design and costumes followed Russell's stage directions. It was performed on a proscenium arch stage, using an eleven-piece orchestra for the music.

2) Most productions have staged *Blood Brothers* in the way that Russell originally intended — the look of the costumes and sets conform to Russell's suggestions or early productions of the play.

3) The play has been performed all over the world in countries such as Denmark, Japan and South Korea — even these international productions have used similar costumes and sets to the original production.

4) However, some productions have staged the play differently to suit the director's dramatic intentions or to emphasise certain messages. In 1997, an unofficial production of *Blood Brothers* was staged in Siberia. This production interpreted the play as a Christian moral tale, so it used a 250-piece choir for the songs.

5) Some productions have used different staging to bring the action closer to the audience — for example, a 2015 production in Australia took place in a small theatre of only 120 seats, and the play opened with the cast walking through the audience to the stage.

6) Most productions of *Blood Brothers* maintain the original story and setting, but in 2013, David Kramer adapted the play for a South African audience:

- The play was set in Cape Town and featured a mostly black cast.
- The dialogue and lyrics were adapted to fit its new setting — for example, references to the Devil were changed to the Tokoloshe, a mischievous sprite in African folklore.
- There was also a different social message — the play showed the oppression of black South Africans during apartheid.

> Apartheid was a system of racial segregation (where people of different races are separated within their community) that was in place in South Africa between 1948 and 1994. This system discriminated against black South Africans.

I went to a theatre convention — it felt a bit staged to me...

Most productions of the play stick to Russell's suggestions, but that doesn't mean you have to. Feel free to get creative in your answers — just make sure you can explain why you've made each of your choices.

Practice Questions

After all that history, we're back in the present — just in time for you to do this lovely page of practice questions. Talk about perfect timing... Work your way through the quick questions to see how much you've remembered. Then move on to the in-depth questions — try to write about a paragraph for each of these.

Quick Questions

1) Give one way that the economic recession affected working-class people in the 1960s and 1970s.

2) Explain what a 'New Town' is.

3) How does Edward benefit from his middle-class upbringing?

4) Give an example from the play where money is used to show a character's power.

5) How does Russell present different family structures in *Blood Brothers*?

6) Give an example of a time when 'youth culture' is reflected in the play.

7) Name three things that have influenced Russell's writing.

8) Give two features of a typical 'megamusical'.

9) When and where was the musical version of *Blood Brothers* first performed?

In-depth Questions

1) Explain how the differences between Liverpool and Skelmersdale might influence your set design.

2) How does Russell present gender roles as damaging in the play?

3) How do Mickey and Edward's character arcs link to the play's themes of growing up and social class?

4) Explain how Russell uses class stereotypes in the play. Why does he do this?

5) How might Russell's upbringing have influenced the plot and setting of *Blood Brothers*?

6) Imagine you are directing a production of the play. Would you stage the play in the same way as the original 1983 production? Explain why/why not.

Practice Questions

Now you've made it through Section One, it's time to practise some exam-style questions. I know you're keen to have a go, but don't leap straight in. The first set of questions are for the AQA exam and the second set are for the OCR exam, so check with your teacher which exam board you're using before you get started.

Exam-style Questions — AQA

AQA and OCR use different types of exam questions — see p.72 for more on this.

> Find the part of Act One where Mrs Lyons takes one of the twins. Read from where "**Mrs Lyons enters, still with the pregnancy padding.**" to where Mrs Lyons exits, then answer Question 1.

1) Imagine you're a costume designer working on a production of *Blood Brothers*. Explain how you would use costume design to create effects that reinforce the action in this extract.

> Find the part of Act One where Mr Lyons gives Edward a toy gun. Read from where "**Edward reaches his home and walks in.**" to where Mr Lyons says "**Must dash.**" Then answer Question 2.

2) Imagine you're a designer working on staging this extract of *Blood Brothers*. Explain how you would use props and stage furniture to portray this extract effectively to the audience. You should explain why your ideas are suitable for this extract and for the rest of the play.

> Find the part of Act One where Mrs Johnstone locks herself in the house. Read from "**Mickey aged seven is knocking incessantly**" to where Mickey says "**Mam, I'm sorry**", then answer Question 3.

3) Imagine you're a designer working on *Blood Brothers*. Discuss how you would use staging and set design to stage this extract effectively for the audience.

Exam-style Questions — OCR

1) Explain how the social and historical context of *Blood Brothers* are reflected in the part of the play where Mr Lyons fires the factory workers in Act Two. Support your answer with examples from the text.

2) Explain how the cultural context of *Blood Brothers* affects the characters in the play. You should discuss two examples from the play in your answer.

Form and Genre

The form of a play is the type of drama it is — *Blood Brothers* is a musical. Genre just refers to the type of story that is being told, such as a tragedy or a comedy. So, will it be sad tears or happy tears? Or both...

'Blood Brothers' is a musical

A musical is a play where music, singing and dancing are key elements. Musicals have three parts — the script, the music and the lyrics. The songs in *Blood Brothers* play a vital part in the production.

1) Russell uses songs to move the action along. For example, during the song 'Miss Jones', the audience sees Mickey get married and also lose his job in the space of a few minutes.

2) Songs are also used to reveal a character's emotions. Many of the songs in *Blood Brothers* act as soliloquies, giving the audience an insight into the character's thoughts. 'Long Sunday Afternoon' reveals how much the brothers miss each other when they are separated, highlighting their strong bond.

3) They also contribute to the atmosphere on stage. At the end of Act One, 'Bright New Day' creates a mood of optimism and hope, reinforcing Mrs Johnstone's happiness at the prospect of moving away.

The play has elements of tragedy...

1) A tragedy is a story based on the downfall of its main character. *Blood Brothers* uses some features of this genre.

2) Like most tragedies, *Blood Brothers* deals with serious themes and has an unhappy ending — this makes it sad for the audience to watch.

3) Many tragedies use a chorus — a group of actors who guide the audience through what's happening on stage. The Narrator fulfils a similar role in *Blood Brothers* — he oversees the action and comments on the choices the characters make.

4) In a tragedy, the downfall of the main character is usually inevitable. The cyclical structure of *Blood Brothers* (see p.18) suggests to the audience that the twins can't escape their fate.

> **Effect on the Audience**
>
> A tragedy should provoke strong emotions in the audience. The release of these emotions is called catharsis. The ending of *Blood Brothers* makes the audience feel sorrow, so they achieve catharsis.

... but it doesn't fit neatly into the tragic genre

1) Tragedies usually end with the death of the main character. However, in *Blood Brothers* several characters suffer a tragic fate — both of the twins die, and Mrs Johnstone and Mrs Lyons both lose children.

2) Traditionally, tragedies feature high-status characters like kings, but Russell focuses on working-class and middle-class characters. This makes the story more relatable and shows that tragedy can happen to anyone.

© Donald Cooper/ photostage

3) *Blood Brothers* also uses features of other genres:

- Comedy — there are many light-hearted moments in the play, such as the twins lying about the film they're going to see in Act Two. This provides comic relief from the play's serious themes.

- Fairy tale — the Narrator takes on the role of a storyteller. He uses language features often found in traditional fairy tales, such as rhyming couplets and repetition of key phrases.

EXAM TIP

Russell really makes a song and dance out of tragedy...

In the exam, you need to be able to explain how the genre and form of *Blood Brothers* might influence the decisions of a director, designer or performer — think about any issues or opportunities they could create.

Structure

Russell plays with structure to make sure the audience feels the full effects of the tragedy unfolding on stage.

'Blood Brothers' has a cyclical structure

1) The beginning of *Blood Brothers* includes a *"re-enactment"* of the end of the play. Opening and closing the play with the same moment creates the impression that the ending can't be avoided.

2) This cyclical structure helps to create dramatic irony (when the audience knows more than the characters on stage). For example, dramatic irony is created when the twins swear to "stand by" each other in Act One, as the audience knows that they will actually die together.

3) Although the play has a cyclical structure, the narrative is mostly linear after the re-enactment of the ending. This helps to build tension — the audience knows that the story is moving towards a fixed point (the twins' deaths), but they don't know exactly when or how it will be reached.

> **Staging**
>
> Russell doesn't specify how much of the ending should be shown in the re-enactment — he just says *"final moments"*. Directors need to decide whether to show the whole ending, a few seconds of it or even just a freeze frame.

The action is continuous and fast-paced

1) Russell condenses the events of more than 20 years into two short acts — there are many sudden time jumps and changes in location throughout the play. This speeds up the action.

2) The pace of the action increases in the second half of Act Two — Russell uses a series of time jumps and short bursts of action to create the impression that the play is accelerating towards its tragic ending.

3) There are no scene breaks in the play — changes in time and location are quick and smooth, and the only break in the story is the interval at the end of Act One. This helps the action to flow, so the audience gets no relief from the play's rapid pace.

> **Lighting Design**
>
> Russell intended for the play's scene changes to be indicated through lighting (see p.50). Lighting designers and directors need to consider how they can use lighting to help the audience follow the play's fast-paced action.

> **Cross-cutting**
>
> • Russell sometimes uses cross-cutting to show two different moments on stage at the same time. This helps to accelerate the pace of the play.
>
> • For example, the moments where Sammy convinces Mickey to help rob the petrol station, and Edward proposes to Linda are staged simultaneously. This makes it seem like events are happening quickly.

© Jeff Busby

This production showed several separate moments on stage at the same time.

My mam always said what goes around, comes around...

Imagine you're directing a production of 'Blood Brothers'. Write a paragraph describing how you'd stage the first and last moments to emphasise the play's cyclical structure. Write about:

1) The effect of emphasising this structure.
2) Any design features you could use to do this.
3) How these features would emphasise the play's cyclical structure to the audience.

> **Tick list:**
> ✓ dramatic intentions
> ✓ design skills
> ✓ effect on audience

Style

This page helps you plan your outfit for the exam. Oh, wait, no... style just means the way a play is staged.

'Blood Brothers' includes some naturalistic elements...

1) Naturalism is a style of theatre that aims to recreate real life on stage. The audience should forget they're watching a play and be able to imagine that what they're seeing on stage is real. There are several features in *Blood Brothers* that make it feel more believable for the audience.

2) *Blood Brothers* is set in real locations (Liverpool and Skelmersdale) — the play tries to replicate real life by making references to real places.

3) Some elements of the play reflect its historical context. Most of the play's characters speak in the way that working-class or middle-class people would have spoken at the time (see p.22), and there are references to costumes that reflect late 20th-century fashions.

4) The events of the play are realistic and reflect real life. The situations the characters face could really happen, making it easier for the audience to suspend their disbelief.

> **Context**
>
> Russell's stage directions mention clothing from the time when the play is set. In Act Two, Mrs Johnstone wears "*overalls*"— a kind of apron that 1960s housewives often wore.

... but it also has non-naturalistic features

Non-naturalistic theatre includes features that remind an audience that what they're watching isn't real. This encourages them to focus on the play's message. There are many non-naturalistic elements within *Blood Brothers*:

- The Narrator breaks the fourth wall (see p.44) by speaking directly to the audience, and his speech contains rhyme and repetition, which makes his dialogue seem less natural.

- The play has a cyclical narrative and there are some flashbacks, e.g when the Judge tells Sammy off. These narrative features make the plot less realistic, which reminds the audience that they're watching a play.

- The Narrator plays other roles (see p.39). This draws the audience's attention to the fact that they're watching characters and not real people.

- The play's musical elements (e.g. singing) don't resemble real life.

Some productions of 'Blood Brothers' choose to use non-naturalistic lighting effects.

© Australian Production 2015 / Produced by Enda Markey / Photograph by Kurt Sneddon

The play is often staged using a mixture of these styles

1) When staging *Blood Brothers*, directors choose the overall style of the production and decide whether they want to use more naturalistic or non-naturalistic features. Many productions combine these styles.

2) The play is intended to be staged using a minimalist set design — the settings aren't reproduced as they would appear in real life (see p.46). However, the set that does exist is often naturalistic, e.g. it accurately represents what the play's locations would have been like in the late 20th century.

3) The play uses lighting in a non-naturalistic way, e.g. to indicate scene changes. However, naturalistic effects can also be created — dim lighting could be used to represent the crowded streets of Liverpool.

4) The same actors often play Mickey, Linda and Edward as children, teenagers and adults. This is a non-naturalistic feature — having adults play children makes the story less believable for the audience.

EXAM TIP

Been caught procrastinating? Just act naturalistic...

It's fine to use a mix of naturalistic and non-naturalistic features in a production of the play — just make sure that you can justify your choices and that you think about the effect they'll have on the audience.

Mood and Atmosphere

One minute there's fun, then there's fear and felonies — *Blood Brothers* is an emotional rollercoaster...

'Blood Brothers' features contrasting moods

1) Russell uses a mixture of <u>serious</u> and <u>humorous</u> moments in the play. This means that the <u>mood</u> on stage <u>shifts</u> throughout the play.

2) However, there is always an <u>underlying</u> sense of <u>tension</u> — the <u>opening</u> of the play reveals to the audience that there will be an <u>unhappy ending</u>. This creates an <u>ominous</u> <u>atmosphere</u> that is <u>maintained</u> throughout the play.

3) The mood is <u>darker</u> in Act Two than in Act One. In Act Two, <u>light-hearted</u> moments are <u>immediately followed</u> by <u>serious</u> ones. This makes any <u>happiness</u> in the characters' lives seem <u>fleeting</u>.

This production uses lighting to enhance the serious mood on stage.

© Australian Production 2015 / Produced by Enda Markey / Photograph by Kurt Sneddon

Elements of performance can reinforce mood and atmosphere

The <u>movement</u>, <u>gestures</u> and <u>actions</u> of characters can <u>create</u> or <u>enhance</u> atmosphere and mood.

- Actors can use performance skills to create <u>comedy</u> in Act One when Mickey tells Edward that Sammy has a <u>plate</u> in his head. Edward sneaking around Sammy to "*get a close look*" would make this moment even more <u>humorous</u> for the audience.

- At the start of Act Two, the audience sees Mrs Johnstone <u>laughing</u> and "*hustling* Mickey *to* <u>school</u>". This portrayal of a <u>happy</u> and <u>normal family life</u> creates a <u>hopeful</u> and <u>optimistic</u> mood on stage.

- Mrs Lyons's violent <u>attack</u> on Mrs Johnstone in Act Two creates a <u>dark</u> and <u>threatening</u> atmosphere. Her <u>aggressive</u> actions are <u>shocking</u> for the audience to witness and make them <u>fearful</u> of Mrs Lyons.

Lighting and sound help to build tension

1) At the start of Act One, the Narrator <u>stands alone</u> on stage before the "*lights come up*" to reveal the <u>re-enactment</u> of the end of the play. Keeping everything on stage apart from the <u>Narrator</u> in complete <u>darkness</u> creates <u>suspense</u> as the audience waits to see what will be <u>revealed</u>. This builds a <u>tense</u> and <u>mysterious</u> atmosphere before the <u>lights</u> are <u>brought up</u> to show the re-enactment.

Lighting Design

Directors can <u>choose</u> how to <u>interpret</u> Russell's stage directions to create <u>different effects</u>. For example, the lights could be raised <u>slowly</u> on the re-enactment, to <u>delay</u> the moment when it is fully revealed, gradually building <u>intrigue</u>, or they could snap on <u>quickly</u> and flood the stage with light to <u>shock</u> the audience.

2) The <u>stage directions</u> often indicate that <u>incidental music</u> should be introduced before <u>tense</u> moments, such as before Mrs Lyons and Mrs Johnstone make their pact. <u>Sound designers</u> can use <u>eerie</u> or <u>unsettling</u> music to <u>signify</u> that something <u>bad</u> is about to happen.

3) <u>Sound effects</u> are also used to build <u>tension</u>. When Mrs Johnstone and Mrs Lyons make their pact, a "*heartbeat*" sound gradually grows <u>louder</u>. This sound is <u>unsettling</u> for the audience — it emphasises Mrs Johnstone's <u>fear</u>, which helps to create an <u>intense</u> and <u>uneasy</u> atmosphere.

EXAM TIP

There are more mood swings than in a GCSE classroom...

When you're writing about acting, directing or design decisions, think about the impact they could have on the mood and atmosphere on stage. Write about the effect these choices might have on the audience.

Stage Directions

Stage directions tell performers and designers when and how to do things — they'd be lost without them...

Stage directions are used in different ways in 'Blood Brothers'

1) Russell uses lots of <u>stage directions</u> in *Blood Brothers* to <u>guide</u> performers and designers. These include instructions on how <u>actors</u> should use <u>speech</u>, <u>movement</u>, <u>facial expressions</u> and <u>gestures</u>, as well as suggestions for <u>design</u> elements, including <u>sound</u>, <u>costume</u>, <u>lighting</u> and <u>props</u>.

2) He also uses stage directions to describe how <u>changes</u> in <u>time</u> and <u>location</u> can be shown.

3) They're used to specify the <u>positioning</u> of actors — either <u>on stage</u> or <u>in relation</u> to <u>one another</u>. These directions often help to <u>convey</u> certain <u>messages</u> to the <u>audience</u>.

4) Some stage directions give a <u>straightforward</u> direction, e.g. "<u>Mickey *bursts in*</u>". Others are more <u>descriptive</u> and open to the actor's <u>interpretation</u>, e.g. "*shoots him <u>like he was eating his breakfast</u>*".

Russell uses stage directions to control the pace of the action

1) Stage directions are used to indicate the <u>timing</u> and <u>order</u> of <u>entrances</u> and <u>exits</u>. This is particularly important in *Blood Brothers*, because the action is supposed to <u>run continuously</u> with <u>no scene breaks</u>.

2) They show how <u>scene changes</u> should occur. Some suggest <u>smooth</u> transitions so that the action <u>flows</u>, e.g. "*the scene <u>fades</u>*". Others advise <u>sudden</u> shifts — "*the scene <u>snaps</u> from Mrs Lyons*".

3) Russell also uses stage directions to indicate <u>pauses</u> in <u>dialogue</u> or <u>action</u> — e.g. when Mickey tells Mrs Johnstone that Linda is <u>pregnant</u>, there is "*A moment*" before the next line of dialogue. This creates <u>tension</u>, as the audience anticipates her <u>reaction</u>.

© Jeff Busby

4) <u>Musical elements</u> are <u>integrated</u> into the play using stage directions. These directions control <u>transitions</u> into songs by indicating when <u>music</u> and <u>singing</u> should begin. Stage directions are also used to <u>choreograph</u> the action so it's <u>in time</u> with the music, e.g. "<u>*punctuated by a note*</u>, Mrs Johnstone *wheels*".

Stage directions are used to choreograph the children's game in Act One.

Stage directions help performers to interpret their characters

Stage directions give actors information about <u>how to perform</u> their characters at certain moments.

1) They can give <u>practical information</u>.	When 'Bright New Day' begins in Act One, stage directions tell performers whether to <u>deliver</u> their lines by "<u>*singing*</u>" or "<u>*speaking*</u>".
2) They can show a character's <u>motivations</u>.	When Mickey, Edward and Linda are playing with Sammy's air pistol in the park, Linda gives Mickey a "<u>*satisfied smile*</u>" when she hits the target. This could hint at her <u>desire</u> to <u>impress</u> or <u>beat Mickey</u>.
3) They can reveal a character's <u>emotions</u>.	At the end of Act Two, Mrs Johnstone runs "<u>*frantically*</u>" after Mickey. This suggests that she's <u>desperately worried</u> about her son's safety.

EXAM TIP

I was lost in the theatre, so I asked for stage directions...

Stage directions provide information that isn't accessible to the audience. It's important that you can explain how actors might interpret stage directions to convey messages and emotions to the audience.

Speech and Language

News flash: speech tends to be a key element to drama. Who knew? But seriously, how a performer delivers lines is just as important as what they say — it can really bring the play's atmosphere and characters to life.

The play uses a mixture of speech, song and rhyme

1) *Blood Brothers* is a musical, so it uses both lyrics and dialogue to convey its story to the audience.

2) The dialogue is usually naturalistic — it contains the kind of language that would be used in a real conversation, e.g. Mrs Johnstone says "Erm, well" when she's uncertain. This makes the character's interactions feel more realistic.

3) Songs are an important non-naturalistic element of the play (see p.17 for more on the purpose of songs in *Blood Brothers*). They are often integrated into the dialogue.

4) Russell also uses other non-naturalistic language features, such as rhyme, chants and repetition. For example, he uses repetition of key lines to reinforce the play's themes — the Narrator repeats the line "the devil's got your number", which emphasises that the characters can't escape their fate.

© Neil J Halin

A character's speech can show their social class...

1) The working-class characters use speech that is typically associated with working-class people in Northern England:

- they use non-standard English — e.g. Mickey says "Gis a sweet." He uses "Gis" instead of "Give me".

- they use dialect words — e.g. the Johnstone children call their mother "Mam".

- they often omit letters from words — e.g. Mickey says "D' they call y' Eddie?"

Context

Russell uses accents to convey the differences between the classes. The working-class characters speak with a regional Liverpudlian accent, whereas middle-class characters use Received Pronunciation, which is more formal.

2) Middle-class characters like the Lyonses speak very differently — they use formal language, Standard English and formal sentence structures, e.g. Mrs Lyons says "I'm finding it rather large at present." This emphasises that they are well educated and reinforces their middle-class status to the audience.

... and it can reveal their personality

1) Sammy's language is often coarse and full of swear words, e.g. "Y' little robbin' get." This emphasises his aggressive personality.

2) In Act One, Mrs Lyons's language is full of commands, which makes her seem confident and authoritative. Later, her speech includes a lot of questions, e.g. "We're safe here, aren't we?" This change in her language emphasises how insecure and anxious she has become.

3) As a child, Linda often speaks in a direct way. She declares her feelings for Mickey in Act Two, saying "I just love you. I love you!" This highlights her bold personality.

Vocal Skills

Performers could use their vocal skills to emphasise these traits. For example, an actor playing Mrs Lyons could deliver commands in a clear and confident tone.

Speech and Language

Relationships are shown through speech and song

1) Russell uses different types of <u>speech</u> to show how his characters <u>feel</u> and how they <u>interact</u>:

- A **DUOLOGUE** is when <u>two characters</u> have a <u>conversation</u> together.
- A **MONOLOGUE** is when a character makes a <u>speech</u> to <u>another character</u> or the <u>audience</u>.
- A **SOLILOQUY** is when a character <u>talks to themselves</u> and the other characters on stage <u>can't hear</u> them. This conveys the character's <u>inner thoughts</u> and <u>feelings</u> to the audience.
- **CHORAL SPEECH** is when several characters say the <u>same thing</u> at the <u>same time</u>.

2) Mrs Johnstone and Edward have a <u>duologue</u> when she gives him the locket in Act One. This creates an <u>intimate atmosphere</u> which shows their <u>close bond</u>.

3) Mickey's <u>monologue</u> where he says "I wish I was our Sammy" reveals his <u>complicated</u> relationship with his older brother to the audience — it shows how Mickey both <u>idolises</u> and <u>resents</u> Sammy.

4) <u>Soliloquies</u> mainly occur in the play as <u>songs</u>. In Act One, the song 'Easy Terms' <u>conveys</u> to the audience the <u>sadness</u> Mrs Johnstone feels about <u>giving</u> away one of her <u>children</u>.

5) <u>Choral speech</u> is used when the children <u>chant</u> at Mickey after he <u>swears</u> in Act One. Speaking in <u>unison</u> highlights that the group are acting <u>together</u> as <u>one force</u> to bully Mickey.

The Narrator's language sets him apart

1) The language used by the Narrator <u>varies</u> throughout the play — sometimes he uses <u>regional dialect</u> and sometimes he speaks <u>formally</u>. This makes him seem <u>classless</u>, as he <u>doesn't fit</u> neatly into any <u>class stereotype</u>.

2) The Narrator also uses <u>non-naturalistic</u> language — he often speaks in <u>rhyming couplets</u>, which highlights his role as the <u>storyteller</u>.

3) He often <u>addresses</u> the <u>audience directly</u> — he <u>invites</u> the audience to "<u>judge</u>" Mrs Johnstone's actions for <u>themselves</u>. This <u>reinforces</u> his role as a storyteller who is delivering a <u>moral tale</u> to the audience.

Genre

This <u>language feature</u> introduces <u>fairytale</u> elements into the play (see p.17).

© David Cooper Photo

Imagery of Superstition

- The Narrator's speech often contains <u>images</u> that are related to <u>superstition</u>, e.g. "a black cat stalking". The superstitions that he refers to are <u>omens</u> of <u>bad luck</u>, so they create a sense of <u>threat</u>.
- The Narrator often references the <u>Devil</u> pursuing certain characters. This creates a feeling of constant <u>danger</u> — the audience are <u>aware</u> of the play's <u>inevitable ending</u>, but don't know <u>when</u> or <u>how</u> it <u>occurs</u>.

REVISION TASK

What do you call a bit of wooden dialogue? Dire-log...

Choose a duologue from the play that isn't on this page. Imagine you are performing one of the characters and write a paragraph about how you would deliver your lines. Write about:

1) What you want to convey about the characters' relationship.
2) The vocal skills you would use to do this.
3) The effect that your choices would have on the audience.

Tick list:
✓ dramatic intentions
✓ vocal skills
✓ effect on audience

Practice Questions

Phew, that was a tough section... But now you know all the tricks of the trade. Before you put your knowledge to good use by writing an international smash-hit musical, have a go at this page of practice questions.

Quick Questions

1) Give three ways that songs are used in the play.

2) How does the play resemble a tragedy? Give two examples.

3) Explain one effect that the play's cyclical structure has on the audience.

4) Give three features of the play that are non-naturalistic.

5) How could lighting be used to build tension in the play's opening moments?

6) Explain how sound effects might be used to create suspense when Mrs Lyons and Mrs Johnstone make their pact in Act One.

7) Give two examples of how Russell uses stage directions to control the pace of the play.

8) What is the effect of actors using regional accents?

9) What is a soliloquy? What effect might a soliloquy have on the audience?

10) Why does Russell include imagery related to superstition in the Narrator's dialogue?

In-depth Questions

1) If you were directing a production of *Blood Brothers*, would you emphasise its naturalistic or non-naturalistic features? Give reasons for your answer.

2) Imagine you are performing the role of the Narrator. Explain how you would use vocal and physical skills in your performance to create a menacing atmosphere for the audience.

3) When Mrs Johnstone is fired by Mrs Lyons in Act One, the stage directions describe her as "***thinking, desperate; trying to get it together***". How might an actor use these directions to help them portray Mrs Johnstone's character to the audience in this part of the play?

4) Write a short paragraph describing one technique Russell uses to create a dark mood in Act One, and explain how this adds to the play's ominous atmosphere.

Practice Questions

Here's a page of lovely exam-style questions as a reward for getting through that section. OK, so 'lovely' might be stretching it ever so slightly, but they'll really help you practise what you've learnt about Russell's techniques.

Exam-style Questions — AQA

To learn more about the AQA and OCR exams, turn to p.72.

> Find the part of Act One where Mrs Lyons fires Mrs Johnstone. Read from where Mrs Lyons says "**Sit down.**" to "**Mrs Lyons turns and walks away**", then answer Question 1.

1) Imagine you're a performer playing Mrs Lyons. Explain how you and the actor playing Mrs Johnstone would use the space on stage and interact with each other to create a threatening atmosphere for the audience.

> Find the part of Act Two where Mickey and Edward have been to the cinema. Read from "**Edward *and* Mickey *emerge from the cinema***" to where the Mate exits, then answer Question 2.

2) Imagine you're a performer playing Edward. Explain how you and the actors playing Mickey, Linda and Linda's Mate would use the space on stage and interact with each other to create humour for the audience.

> Find the part of Act Two where the Policemen shoot Mickey. Read from "**Nobody move, please.**" to the end of the play, then answer Question 3.

3) Imagine you're a lighting designer working on the play. Explain how you would use lighting to portray this extract effectively on stage for the audience. You should refer to the tragic elements of the play in your answer.

Exam-style Questions — OCR

1) Write a comparison of the advantages and disadvantages a director might face when using an entirely naturalistic set design in *Blood Brothers*.

2) Explain how a performer playing Mickey might use stage directions to help him convey his character when the audience is introduced to seven-year-old Mickey in Act One.

3) How might a director stage the opening of Act Two to make it engaging for the audience? Explain how they might direct the design of this part of the play.

Character Performance — Mrs Johnstone

This section is jam-packed with handy suggestions for performing each of the main characters in the play. It starts with Mrs Johnstone — an adoring mother whose sons give her plenty of grief from start to finish.

Mrs Johnstone is a single mother

1) Mrs Johnstone is a <u>working-class</u> mother. At the start of the play, she works as a <u>cleaner</u> for the Lyonses.

2) She <u>worries</u> a lot about <u>money</u>, so she is <u>relieved</u> to have a job — it means that she "can just manage to get by". She <u>works hard</u> to provide for her children, but she still wishes she could give them a <u>better life</u>.

3) As a working-class woman in a society where <u>men</u> hold most of the <u>power</u>, she is often <u>vulnerable</u> to <u>authority</u> figures or people from a <u>higher social class</u> — she feels <u>helpless</u> against the debt collectors and is <u>easily manipulated</u> by Mrs Lyons.

© Nils Jorgensen/REX/Shutterstock

> **Mrs Johnstone is...**
>
> **superstitious:** "Mrs Lyons, never put new shoes on a table..."
> **vulnerable:** "How are we gonna live without my job?"
> **caring:** "Does your mother look after you?"

She struggles to support her family

1) When she was <u>younger</u>, Mrs Johnstone's life was <u>carefree</u>. She has <u>happy memories</u> of going <u>dancing</u> and <u>enjoying</u> herself. When she got <u>pregnant</u>, she had to get <u>married</u> and take on adult <u>responsibilities</u>.

2) At the start of the play, she already has <u>seven children</u>. She is raising them <u>alone</u> because her husband <u>left her</u> for another woman. When she finds out she's expecting <u>twins</u>, she knows she <u>can't support</u> two more children.

3) Throughout the play, Mrs Johnstone's character arc is linked to the life of <u>Marilyn Monroe</u>. She wants her life to be <u>fun</u> and <u>glamorous</u> like Monroe's, but the audience can see that her life is destined to end in <u>tragedy</u>.

> **Context**
>
> Monroe was one of the most <u>famous</u> Hollywood stars of the 1950s. People believed she lived a very <u>glamorous</u> and <u>carefree</u> lifestyle, but in <u>private</u> she struggled with <u>mental health issues</u> and <u>substance abuse</u>. She died aged 36 from an <u>overdose</u>.

> **Effect on the Audience**
>
> Mr Johnstone <u>never appears</u> on stage. His absence highlights Mrs Johnstone's <u>isolation</u> and her <u>lack of support</u>, which encourages the audience to feel <u>sympathy</u> for her.

She's a very maternal character

1) Even though they cause her lots of <u>stress</u>, Mrs Johnstone is <u>devoted</u> to her children.

2) She is <u>compassionate</u> towards her children and <u>understands</u> their feelings — she sees early on that Mickey has <u>feelings</u> for Linda, and she <u>supports</u> him when he tells her Linda is <u>pregnant</u>.

3) She <u>openly</u> shows <u>affection</u> for her children — she <u>hugs</u> and <u>kisses</u> Mickey throughout the play. She <u>worries</u> about showing that she <u>cares</u> for Edward in case Mrs Lyons finds out, but she still "<u>cradles</u>" him when he's upset about moving to Skelmersdale.

4) Even her decision to give Edward away is motivated by <u>love</u> for her <u>children</u>. She doesn't <u>want</u> to give a baby to Mrs Lyons, but she does it because she thinks he'll have a <u>better life</u> with the Lyonses. She also knows she will struggle to <u>look after</u> the rest of her children if she keeps both twins.

5) Although she is a loving mother, she isn't always a <u>responsible</u> parent — for example, she <u>excuses</u> Sammy's <u>worsening behaviour</u>, saying "it's very easily done" when he burns the school down.

Character Performance — Mrs Johnstone

She looks older than she really is

At the start of the play, Mrs Johnstone *"is aged thirty but looks more like fifty"* — she's worn out from caring for her children and working hard to support her family. This could be reflected in her physical appearance:

- An actor might use a slightly hunched posture, as if Mrs Johnstone is physically weighed down by the pressure of supporting her family. This could attract sympathy from the audience.
- A director might cast an older actor, but a younger actor could use facial expressions to make her look older. For example, she might use a weary expression to make her look drained of energy.

She's optimistic but vulnerable in Act One

© Donald Cooper/ photostage

1) Despite her difficult life, Mrs Johnstone is hopeful about her future in Act One. She says that "now I've got me a little job we'll be OK".

2) Her financial situation means that she is easily manipulated by more powerful characters like Mrs Lyons — she is persuaded by Mrs Lyons's arguments that she should give one of the twins away.

3) At the end of Act One, Mrs Johnstone is excited to move to Skelmersdale where her family "can begin again".

Act One — Physical Skills

- Mrs Johnstone might shrink away when Mrs Lyons hugs her to suggest that she is unhappy about the choice she has made.
- She could spread her arms wide to show her confidence and excitement when she tells her children about the things they'll be able to afford when she has a job.

Act One — Vocal Skills

- She could use a high pitch and a desperate tone to say "The welfare have already been on to me" to highlight her vulnerability.
- When she says the line "We'll live like kings", she could speak slowly and softly — this would give the impression that she's daydreaming about a better future.

She gains confidence at the start of Act Two

1) At the start of Act Two, Mrs Johnstone is happy with her new life in Skelmersdale.

2) She becomes more defiant and is determined to protect her new life — this gives her the confidence to stand up to Mrs Lyons when she confronts her about the locket.

Act Two — Physical Skills

- An actor could use quick, energetic movements when Mrs Johnstone and the Milkman *"dance"* to make her seem younger and carefree. She could use a broad smile to show she's happy.
- When she stands up to Mrs Lyons, she could stand up straight and raise her chin — this confident posture would show that she isn't afraid of Mrs Lyons and that she isn't going to back down.

Act Two — Vocal Skills

- When her lines get *"Slower"* at the start of Act Two, she could use a sad and serious tone — this would show that even though her life is happy, there are still things that worry her.
- She might speak loudly and steadily as she says "I'm stayin' here. You move if you want to." She could place emphasis on "stayin'" to show her determination not to give in to Mrs Lyons.

Character Performance — Mrs Johnstone

She loses hope towards the end of Act Two

1) In the second half of Act Two, Mrs Johnstone feels <u>helpless</u> — she is <u>unable</u> to <u>protect</u> Mickey as his life spirals out of control. She is <u>relieved</u> when Linda says she's got Mickey a job, but this doesn't last.

2) She is <u>devastated</u> at the end of the play when Mickey <u>blames</u> her for how his life turned out and both twins are <u>killed</u> — she wishes it was "just a story" and doesn't want to <u>believe</u> that her sons are <u>dead</u>.

Act Two — Physical Skills

- An actor might use <u>tense body language</u> to show how <u>worried</u> she is about Mickey and then <u>relax</u> as she says "thank God" — this would suggest a <u>weight</u> has been <u>lifted</u> from her shoulders.
- When the twins die, she could <u>fall to her knees</u> to show her <u>horror</u> and <u>despair</u>. She could <u>reach out</u> towards them and <u>lean over</u> their bodies as though she is still trying to <u>protect</u> them.

Act Two — Vocal Skills

- She could use a <u>desperate tone</u> and speak <u>slowly</u> as she tells Linda, "We've gorra do somethin' about him." to show how <u>tired</u> and <u>hopeless</u> she feels.
- After the twins die, she could sing <u>quietly</u> and use <u>pauses</u> to show how <u>broken</u> she feels.
- She could place <u>emphasis</u> on words like "story" and "dream" — this would highlight that she doesn't want to believe what has happened is <u>real</u>.

© David Cooper Photo

This actor clutches at her coat to show Mrs Johnstone's grief.

In the exam, link performance suggestions to the text

The <u>sample answer</u> below shows how you might write about <u>performing Mrs Johnstone</u> on stage:

> This clearly focuses on a <u>specific moment</u>.

> This considers how <u>performance</u> could support <u>characterisation</u>.

> This <u>develops</u> the point further.

In Act One when the Policeman warns Mrs Johnstone about Mickey's behaviour, she "*shakes her head*" and "*nods*" instead of making a verbal reply. I would make these movements small and quick. This would show that Mrs Johnstone is intimidated by the Policeman and wants to avoid provoking him. I would also bow my head and keep my eyes lowered to look submissive to show that Mrs Johnstone respects the Policeman's authority.

REVISION TASK

Character in a play wishes her life was a story #irony...

Imagine you're directing a production of 'Blood Brothers'. Write performance instructions for the actor playing Mrs Johnstone when she faces the debt collectors in Act One. Think about:

1) Which aspects of Mrs Johnstone's backstory are important?
2) How might the actor interpret Mrs Johnstone's character using a range of physical and vocal performance skills?
3) How does Mrs Johnstone interact with other characters?

Tick list:
✓ background information
✓ physical and vocal skills
✓ interaction with others

Character Performance — Mrs Lyons

Mrs Lyons is the closest thing the play has to a villain — a well-dressed, well-spoken master of manipulation. At the start of Act One, it seems like she's on top of the world, but things soon come crashing down...

Mrs Lyons's wealth doesn't make her happy

© David Cooper Photo

1) Mrs Lyons fulfils the role of a typical middle-class woman in the 1960s — she is a housewife who stays at home while her husband works.

2) The Lyonses have a comfortable lifestyle. Mr Lyons earns a lot of money as a successful businessman, so they live in a "rather large" house in a wealthy area. They can afford to hire Mrs Johnstone to clean it for them.

3) However, Mrs Lyons's life isn't perfect. She and Mr Lyons can't have children, so she spends her time alone while her husband is at work.

4) Taking Edward from Mrs Johnstone doesn't solve Mrs Lyons's problems. She's paranoid about him (or anyone else) finding out the truth, and she goes to extreme lengths to make sure this never happens.

Mrs Lyons is an antagonist — her desperate attempts to protect her secret cause harm to the play's main protagonists: Mrs Johnstone, Mickey and Edward.

Mrs Lyons is...

unhappy: "We've been trying for such a long time now..."
manipulative: "Surely, it's better to give one child to me."
insecure: "I don't want her to hold the baby, Richard."

She is desperate to be a mother

Mrs Lyons's backstory is a key part of her characterisation.

1) Mr and Mrs Lyons assumed that they would have children, but they tried "for such a long time" and weren't able to. Mrs Lyons wanted to adopt but her husband didn't.

2) She feels like a failure because she doesn't have any children — traditionally, women were expected to become mothers (see p.10 for more on traditional gender roles).

3) Mrs Lyons's desire for a child motivates her actions at the start of the play — she manipulates Mrs Johnstone into giving her one of the twins.

4) She is sure that she would be a good mother — at the start of Act One, she presents herself as loving and maternal and she assures Mrs Johnstone she'd "always be there" for her child. She says she would buy her child everything he needed — she thinks giving a child material things makes you a good mother.

She's an unstable character

Effect on the Audience

If an actor chooses to emphasise how lonely Mrs Lyons is, the audience might feel sorry for her at the start of Act One. If an actor highlights Mrs Lyons's manipulative behaviour, the audience might respond more harshly to her.

1) Becoming a mother doesn't make Mrs Lyons happy — she becomes terrified of losing Edward. This makes her over-protective and possessive of him.

2) She becomes "*agitated*" when Mrs Johnstone is near Edward. When she fires Mrs Johnstone, she behaves aggressively and "*roughly drags*" her away from the cot.

3) She reacts furiously when Edward swears at her — she shouts at him and even hits him. When she sees the "*terror*" in his face, she becomes loving and motherly. This sudden change in her behaviour would be unsettling for the audience, and it shows how unpredictable she is.

4) Mrs Lyons becomes more unstable as the play goes on. She attacks Mrs Johnstone with a knife, and later tells Mickey about Edward and Linda's affair to try to split them up.

Character Performance — Mrs Lyons

Her social status gives her power

1) Mrs Lyons's <u>appearance</u> should reflect her <u>high social status</u> and distinguish her from <u>Mrs Johnstone</u>.

2) This is partly the responsibility of the casting director and costume designer (see p.57-58) — for example, a director might cast an actor with a <u>strong build</u> to suggest Mrs Lyons is in <u>good health</u>. However, an actor can also contribute to the character's appearance using <u>physical performance skills</u>.

3) Russell doesn't describe Mrs Lyons's <u>height</u> or <u>build</u>, but an actor might use an <u>upright posture</u> to make her seem <u>taller</u> than Mrs Johnstone. This would make her seem <u>self-assured</u> and <u>authoritative</u>.

4) Her wealth and position in society might give her <u>confidence</u> — she might use <u>decisive movements</u> or <u>maintain eye contact</u> with other characters in order to convey this.

She's manipulative and controlling in Act One

1) Mrs Lyons is <u>gentle</u> and <u>persuasive</u> when she <u>manipulates</u> Mrs Johnstone at the start of Act One. Later, she becomes more <u>threatening</u> and plays on Mrs Johnstone's <u>fears</u> to keep her away from Edward.

2) However, she isn't <u>completely</u> in <u>control</u> of her emotions. During Act One, she becomes more <u>superstitious</u> and grows <u>increasingly afraid</u> of Mrs Johnstone's influence over Edward.

Act One — Physical Skills

- An actor might use <u>open body language</u> to persuade Mrs Johnstone that she can be <u>trusted</u> when she says "you'd be able to see him every day". She might use <u>controlled</u>, <u>careful movements</u> to make her idea seem <u>sensible</u>.
- When she <u>lies</u> about the superstition that the twins will die if they find out the truth, she might use a <u>strong posture</u> and <u>stand close</u> to Mrs Johnstone to try to <u>intimidate</u> her.

Act One — Vocal Skills

- When Mrs Lyons says "Quickly, quickly, tell me", she might <u>interrupt</u> Mrs Johnstone <u>calmly</u> but <u>firmly</u>. This would show that she is <u>controlling</u> the conversation.
- When she says "they shall both immediately die", she could speak at a <u>regular pace</u> — this would suggest that <u>lying</u> to Mrs Johnstone comes <u>naturally</u> to Mrs Lyons.

She becomes more anxious and fearful in Act Two

1) At the start of Act Two, Mrs Lyons still feels <u>insecure</u> in her position as Edward's <u>mother</u> — she needs his <u>reassurance</u> that they've had a nice holiday together.

2) When Mrs Lyons finds out about the <u>locket</u>, she is <u>shaken</u> and <u>upset</u>. Even after so many years, she is <u>afraid</u> of <u>losing</u> him to Mrs Johnstone.

Act Two — Physical Skills

- She could <u>look into Edward's eyes</u> and use a <u>concerned expression</u> as she says "Look after yourself, my love." This would show how <u>deeply</u> she fears for Edward, making her <u>anxiety</u> seem more <u>intense</u> to the audience.
- When she asks him about the locket, she could quickly <u>step towards</u> him and <u>reach out</u> for his shoulders to show she is <u>possessive</u> of him.

An actor clutches her stomach to suggest worry.

Act Two — Vocal Skills

- An actor could use <u>rising inflection</u> as she says "We're safe here, aren't we?" — this would make her sound <u>uncertain</u> and <u>desperate</u> for Edward's reassurance.
- When she says, "but I'm your mother", she could place <u>emphasis</u> on "I'm" as though she's trying to <u>reassure</u> herself that it's true. This would highlight her <u>insecurity</u> to the audience.

Character Performance — Mrs Lyons

She eventually has a breakdown

1) In Act Two, Mrs Lyons becomes increasingly unstable and aggressive — she is unable to cope with her fear of the truth being discovered. She confronts Mrs Johnstone over the locket and attacks her.

2) The last time Mrs Lyons appears in the play is when she shows Mickey that Edward and Linda are together. She doesn't speak during this moment — she has become a shadow of the character she was in Act One.

Act Two — Vocal Skills

- When she asks, "How long have you lived here?" her voice might shake to show she is emotional and unstable.

- When she says, "I curse you. Witch!" she could increase the volume and use a higher pitch to make it sound like she's shrieking — this would highlight that Mrs Lyons has lost control.

Act Two — Physical Skills

- She could stand very still as she and Mrs Johnstone "stare at each other" — this would contrast with her aggression later in the scene and make her seem unpredictable.

- An actor could use jittery movements as she "turns Mickey round and points out Edward and Linda" — this would reinforce her erratic behaviour.

© Donald Cooper/ photostage

Effect on the Audience

Mrs Lyons's behaviour has the potential to create suspense for the audience. If the actor makes it obvious that she's slowly losing control, it will keep the audience guessing at what she'll do next.

Use specific details to write about character performance

Take a look at this sample answer — it shows how you could write about performing Mrs Lyons on stage:

> This makes a clear point and explains its effect on the audience.

> When Mrs Johnstone coos over Edward in Act One, the stage directions say that Mrs Lyons is "obviously agitated". I would wring my hands together and shift from foot to foot to show the audience how anxious and uneasy I feel. I would move quickly and step firmly in between Mrs Johnstone and the cot — this would show my determination to keep her away from Edward. I would use an emphatic tone and speak quickly when she says "He doesn't want to be picked up" to show Mrs Lyons is possessive over Edward and wants to assert authority over Mrs Johnstone.

> This develops the point further.

> This demonstrates good knowledge of Mrs Lyons's backstory.

REVISION TASK

Mrs L's like the leaning tower of Pisa — highly unstable...

Read Act One from "There's nothing wrong with my nerves" to where Mrs Lyons sweeps the shoes off the table. Write a paragraph about how you would perform Mrs Lyons here, including:

1) How you would interact with Mr Lyons.
2) Which vocal and physical skills you might use to convey her feelings.
3) How the audience might react to you.

Tick list:
- ✓ character interaction
- ✓ physical and vocal skills
- ✓ effect on the audience

Character Performance — Mickey Johnstone

Mickey Johnstone's a really nice lad who gets caught up in circumstances that are beyond his control.

Mickey Johnstone is a victim of class division

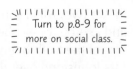

Turn to p.8-9 for more on social class.

1) Mickey is the youngest of Mrs Johnstone's children. He's close to his mother, but he's often picked on by his older siblings — especially Sammy (see p.37).

© Nils Jorgensen/REX/Shutterstock

2) He is from a working-class family and this shapes the rest of his life — he gets a poor education at school which means he has to work a low-paid job. When he is made redundant, he has to live off benefits.

3) He seems happy as a child, but as he gets older, he faces more difficulties in his life and has to grow up quickly.

Mickey is...

friendly: "Do you wanna be my blood brother, Eddie?"

sensitive: "He couldn't stop the tears."

troubled: "Now give me the tablets... I need them."

He's mischievous but caring

1) Mickey cares about his family and friends and wants other people to like him. He pretends to be rebellious and confident, but this is mostly for show.

2) As a child, he is a bad influence on Edward — he teaches him to swear and encourages him to throw stones at a window. However, he also accepts Edward even though he's different and defends him when Sammy calls him a "friggin' poshy".

Effect on the Audience

The audience's response to Mickey's fate depends on how he's presented earlier in the play. The actor can attract sympathy from the audience by highlighting Mickey's positive qualities — this will make him seem more like a victim.

3) As a teenager, he has a clear sense of right and wrong, and he tries to make Sammy pay the correct fare on the bus. He understands the consequences of Sammy's actions and doesn't want to make the same mistakes. He talks back to the teacher, but only because he is struggling at school.

4) He is a loving son to Mrs Johnstone. He's pleased when they move to Skelmersdale because he hasn't seen her "happy like this for ages". As an adult, he's grateful to Mrs Johnstone for letting him live with her. He is sensitive to her feelings and reassures her when she worries that she hasn't given him "much of a life".

He ages over the course of the play

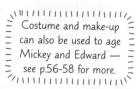

Costume and make-up can also be used to age Mickey and Edward — see p.56-58 for more.

1) Mickey is seven years old when he appears in Act One, but he's a young man at the end of Act Two. He's typically played by the same actor throughout the play.

2) A director might cast an actor with a slight build so that the audience find him more believable when he's playing a child. An actor could also use a range of performance skills to show that Mickey is growing up:

- An actor could alter the pitch of his voice — it might get lower as Mickey gets older.
- He might emphasise Mickey's youthfulness in Act One by moving constantly to make him seem energetic and excitable. Later on, he might use slower, more considered movements to show that he has become more mature.
- Mickey's facial expressions might become less exaggerated and more serious as an adult.

Character Performance — Mickey Johnstone

He's lively and outgoing as a child

1) In Act One, Mickey is a spirited and cheerful boy who enjoys playing with Linda and Edward.

2) He tells Edward that he's been caught by the police "loads of times", but he's lying to seem rebellious and impress Edward. He doesn't really want to get into trouble and cries when the Policeman catches them.

Act One — Physical Skills
- While he's boasting to Edward, an actor could use a straight posture to make himself look tall and confident.

Act One — Vocal Skills
- An actor could speak at a loud volume when he describes his rebellious behaviour and put stress on "loads" to make him sound confident.

He becomes more insecure as a teenager...

In the first half of Act Two, Mickey becomes more self-conscious as he gets older. He develops feelings for Linda but is too awkward to admit it, and he's defensive when Mrs Johnstone teases him about it.

Act Two — Physical Skills
- An actor could move away from Mrs Johnstone as she is *"hustling"* him to school to show that he's embarrassed by her fussing.
- When Mrs Johnstone teases him about having feelings for Linda, he could scowl at her to show he is *"outraged"*. He might also avoid eye contact with her to show that she is right.

© Donald Cooper/ photostage

Act Two — Vocal Skills
- When he says "That was — a line out the school play!" an actor could draw out the pause in the line to suggest that Mickey is struggling to make up an explanation. He could speak the rest of the line after the pause at a fast pace to show that Mickey is hastily trying to defend himself.

... and he resents his lack of opportunities as an adult

1) When Mickey loses his job in the second half of Act Two, his life begins to fall apart. His behaviour becomes unpredictable as he turns to crime, develops depression and quickly becomes addicted to anti-depressants. He eventually has an emotional breakdown.

2) He is angry that Edward has a much better life than he does, saying "how come you got everything... an' I got nothin'?"

Act Two — Vocal Skills
- Mickey's tone might be bitter to show that he's jealous of Edward.
- An actor could place emphasis on "everything" and "nothin'" by spitting them out with aggression — this would show his anger at how different their lives are.

Act Two — Physical Skills
- Mickey's holding a gun at the end of the play — an actor might wave it around wildly to show that he's out of control.
- He could also use tense body language and twitchy gestures to show how unstable Mickey has become.

Hey Mickey, you're actually not so fine...
Mickey changes from a carefree child to a depressed adult over the course of the play. In the exam, you might write about what performance skills an actor could use to convey this change to the audience.

Character Performance — Edward Lyons

Edward Lyons is one complex character — on the one hand, he's a friendly and considerate young man, but on the other, he selfishly betrays his best friend. This is going to take some serious performance skills...

Edward Lyons has a privileged upbringing

1) Edward is the child that Mrs Johnstone <u>gives away</u>. He's raised as the <u>only child</u> of a <u>middle-class couple</u>, rather than growing up in a <u>large</u>, <u>working-class family</u>. This means that his lifestyle is more <u>comfortable</u>.

2) His upbringing with Mr Lyons and Mrs Lyons gives him access to a <u>better education</u> than Mickey, which allows him to go to <u>university</u> and get a <u>good job</u> when he's <u>older</u>.

© David Cooper Photo

3) However, Edward doesn't have an entirely <u>happy</u> upbringing. The Lyonses are <u>strict</u> with him, which makes him want to <u>rebel</u> through his friendship with Mickey. Mr Lyons is a fairly <u>absent</u> father and Mrs Lyons can be <u>unpredictable</u> — she <u>hits</u> Edward in Act One. As an adult, he <u>doesn't</u> seem to have a <u>close relationship</u> with his parents.

Edward is...

generous: "Yes, of course. Take as many as you want."
polite: "You're looking very well, Mrs Johnstone."
naive: "Why don't you buy a new house near us?"

He adapts his behaviour to suit different situations

1) As a child, he is <u>impressionable</u> and tries to <u>copy</u> things that Mickey does — he <u>swears</u> at Mrs Lyons and <u>talks back</u> to the Policeman. He quickly adopts Mickey's <u>superstitions</u> about magpies, and Mrs Lyons worries about the <u>influence</u> Mickey has had on him.

2) As a teenager, he is quite <u>serious</u> and <u>formal</u> when he's with Mrs Lyons. When he's around Mickey and Linda, he is more <u>outgoing</u> — he chats about <u>girls</u>, <u>dances</u> with Linda's Mate and climbs up a <u>lamp post</u>.

3) As an adult, his ability to <u>behave differently</u> in different situations helps him to <u>succeed</u> in life. At the end of the play, he speaks and acts <u>formally</u> as he gives a speech in the town hall — this behaviour is <u>appropriate</u> for his job as a <u>town councillor</u>.

Effect on the Audience

Edward wants to be <u>like</u> Mickey, but they are already <u>more alike</u> than he realises — they're twins. This <u>dramatic irony</u> makes it <u>humorous</u> for the audience to see Edward trying to <u>copy</u> Mickey's behaviour.

He's a child in Act One and grows up in Act Two

1) Edward and Mickey are <u>twins</u> and this could be hinted at through their performance. Actors could use <u>similar mannerisms</u> to make the brothers seem more <u>alike</u>.

2) Like Mickey (see p.32), Edward ages from a <u>seven-year-old boy</u> to a <u>young man</u> during the play. In Act One, an actor might use a slightly <u>hunched posture</u> to make Edward seem <u>shorter</u> and reflect that he is a <u>child</u>. In Act Two, an actor could <u>stand tall</u> to suggest Edward has <u>grown</u>.

Context

In Act One, Edward is presented as a <u>stereotype</u> of a middle-class child in the late 20th century — he is <u>well behaved</u>, <u>articulate</u> and <u>formal</u>.

3) The <u>changes</u> in his behaviour might be more <u>subtle</u> than in Mickey's — Edward has had a <u>strict upbringing</u> and might behave like an <u>adult</u> even when he's a child. For example, an actor might <u>sit still</u> and <u>not fidget</u>, or <u>shake hands</u> when he first meets people to show that he has similar <u>manners</u> to an adult.

Character Performance — Edward Lyons

He's friendly and generous as a child

Edward is <u>eager</u> to talk to Mickey when they first meet in Act One — he approaches him and <u>confidently</u> asks to be <u>friends</u>. He's happy to <u>offer</u> him a <u>sweet</u> and even encourages him to <u>share</u> them with Sammy.

Act One — Physical Skills

- An actor might <u>smile</u> and use <u>excited facial expressions</u> to show he is pleased to meet Mickey.
- He could use <u>enthusiastic gestures</u> like <u>nodding</u> his head when he says "Take as many as you want."

Act One — Vocal Skills

- When he offers Mickey the <u>sweets</u>, he could <u>place emphasis</u> on words like "many" and "want" to highlight his <u>generosity</u> to the audience.
- An actor might use an <u>excited tone</u> when he says "Do you want to come and play?" — this would show how <u>keen</u> he is to be friends with Mickey.

He's torn between two lives as a teenager...

1) Edward still wears Mrs Johnstone's <u>locket</u> in Act Two, which shows that he still <u>cares</u> about her and Mickey. He's also <u>pleased</u> to see her again.

2) However, he also <u>cares</u> about Mrs Lyons and is <u>concerned</u> when she <u>reacts strangely</u> to seeing the picture that's inside the locket.

© David Fisher/REX/Shutterstock

Physical Skills — Act Two

- When he says "Hi-ya, Mrs Johnstone", an actor could <u>smile fondly</u> to show that Edward feels a <u>strong bond</u> with her.
- He could <u>move quickly</u> when he holds Mrs Lyons "*steady*" — this would show he <u>reacts</u> as soon as he sees she's <u>upset</u>.

Vocal Skills — Act Two

- He might use a <u>thoughtful tone</u> when he says "She's fabulous your ma", as if he is <u>imagining</u> what it would be like to be Mrs Johnstone's son.
- When he says "Mummy, what's wrong?" he could use a <u>fast pace</u> to show his <u>surprise</u> and <u>concern</u>.

... but he grows up more slowly than Mickey

1) In Act Two, Edward gets caught up in his life at <u>university</u> and is <u>insensitive</u> when Mickey explains that he is <u>unemployed</u>.

2) When Edward is shown as Councillor Lyons at the end of the play, he is more <u>mature</u> and <u>serious</u> — he displays the kind of <u>middle-class identity</u> that Mrs Lyons wanted him to have.

Physical Skills — Act Two

- When Edward talks about university, an actor could <u>wave his hands</u> around to show that he's <u>excited</u>. This would suggest that he <u>hasn't noticed</u> Mickey's <u>subdued</u> behaviour.
- When he's speaking at the town hall, he could use a <u>confident posture</u> and <u>central stage position</u> to make him seem <u>superior</u>.

Vocal Skills — Act Two

- When he describes how much he's <u>enjoying</u> university, he might place <u>emphasis</u> on words like "fantastic" and "parties" — this would make it sound like he's <u>boasting</u>.
- As a councillor, he might <u>exaggerate</u> Edward's <u>posh accent</u> to show that he's <u>out of touch</u> with the <u>working class</u>.

EXAM TIP

Don't throw Edward to the Lyons...

Edward isn't perfect — he makes some mistakes, but he does plenty of good things too. When you're writing about him, think about how an actor might convey his positive qualities as well as his flaws.

Character Performance — Linda

Linda's an interesting character to perform — she gets a pretty rough deal in life and really tries to make the best of it. Messing around with your husband's twin brother probably isn't the road to happiness, though...

Linda is friends with Mickey and Edward

© Donald Cooper/ photostage

1) Linda is Mickey's <u>childhood friend</u>. She becomes good <u>friends</u> with Edward too, but as an adult she is <u>torn</u> between the two brothers.

> **Linda is...**
>
> **protective:** "Oh leave him alone, you. Y'big worm!"
> **passionate:** "I don't care who knows. I just love you."
> **proactive:** "I think I've got Mickey a job".

2) As a child, she <u>defies</u> many traditional <u>gender roles</u> — she <u>speaks her mind</u>, <u>defends</u> Mickey and plays the <u>same games</u> as the <u>boys</u>.

3) However, she increasingly <u>conforms</u> to gender roles as she gets <u>older</u>. She gets <u>pregnant</u> when she's still a <u>teenager</u> and has to focus on taking care of her <u>family</u> — she follows the <u>same path</u> as Mrs Johnstone.

She's bold and loyal in Act One...

1) As a child, Linda is <u>outspoken</u> and <u>brave</u>. When she <u>stands up</u> to Sammy in Act One, an actor might use a <u>mocking tone</u> when she says "I stopped it with the bin lid" to show that she <u>isn't afraid</u> of Sammy.

2) She is a <u>loyal friend</u> to Mickey and <u>defends</u> him when the other children laugh at him. An actor could highlight Linda's <u>boldness</u> in this moment through <u>performance</u>:

- She might stand <u>in between</u> Mickey and Sammy with a <u>defiant stance</u>. This use of <u>proxemics</u> and <u>body language</u> would make her seem <u>protective</u> of Mickey.
- She could also <u>maintain eye contact</u> with Sammy to appear <u>authoritative</u>.

... but she becomes tired and frustrated in Act Two

1) As a teenager, Linda is <u>bubbly</u> and <u>outgoing</u> — before Edward leaves for university, she <u>jokes</u> with him — "looking for a good time? Ten to seven." As she says the line, an actor could use a <u>light tone</u> of voice and a <u>cheeky facial expression</u> to show Linda's sense of <u>humour</u>.

2) When she gets <u>pregnant</u>, her life becomes more <u>serious</u> — she has to get <u>married</u> and take on <u>adult responsibilities</u>. She <u>struggles</u> to <u>help</u> Mickey when he goes to <u>prison</u> and develops an <u>addiction</u> to <u>pills</u>. An actor could speak <u>quietly</u> as she says "You promised" to show how <u>helpless</u> she feels.

3) She feels <u>trapped</u> by her life with Mickey — she could <u>increase</u> the <u>pace</u> and <u>volume</u> of her voice as she says "An' what about what I need?" to show her <u>frustration</u>.

4) When Linda spends time with Edward, she feels <u>free</u> from her <u>responsibilities</u>. An actor might show this by using <u>cheerful facial expressions</u> and <u>relaxed body language</u>.

> **Effect on the Audience**
>
> The audience might <u>forgive</u> Linda for having an affair if an actor emphasises how <u>unhappy</u> she is with Mickey — this would encourage <u>sympathy</u> for her.

EXAM TIP

The least Linda deserves is affair trial...

Linda has plenty of reasons for behaving the way she does — when you're writing about her, think about how an actor might convey her motivations to make the audience understand why she betrays Mickey.

Character Performance — Sammy Johnstone

What's that? One of your classmates is a troublemaker? Well, Sammy Johnstone is the role for them.

Sammy always gets into trouble

1) Sammy is Mickey's <u>older brother</u>. He <u>bullies</u> Mickey, but Mickey still <u>looks up</u> to him as a <u>role model</u>.

2) He's <u>badly-behaved</u> as a child and his behaviour gets <u>worse</u> during the play — he eventually becomes a <u>criminal</u>. His behaviour goes mostly <u>unpunished</u> in Act One, but he has to face the <u>consequences</u> of his actions in Act Two.

> **Sammy is...**
>
> **aggressive:** "Now move, you. Move! Give me the bag."
> **badly-behaved:** "Sammy burnt the school down"
> **persuasive:** "Fifty quid, Mickey. Fifty quid for an hour's work."

3) As an adult, Sammy is <u>unemployed</u> — he doesn't try to find a job like Mickey, preferring to remain on the "dole". He wants to have <u>money</u> but doesn't want to <u>earn</u> it legally.

He's threatening and abusive in Act One...

1) Sammy is <u>older</u> than Mickey, Edward and Linda, so he's likely to be <u>taller</u> than them — an actor could use an <u>upright posture</u> to emphasise this. This would also make Sammy seem more <u>intimidating</u>.

2) The other children <u>follow Sammy's lead</u> when he starts <u>bullying</u> Mickey. This could be because they are <u>frightened</u> of Sammy. An actor could use a <u>loud volume</u> and a <u>firm tone</u> when he says "Come on, gang, let's go" — this would make him seem <u>controlling</u>.

3) When Linda stands up to him, he could use <u>fidgety body language</u> or a <u>menacing facial expression</u> to suggest that he's <u>short-tempered</u> and likely to react <u>violently</u>.

... and things only get worse in Act Two

1) Sammy doesn't change much as a <u>character</u> over the course of the play, but his <u>behaviour</u> gets more <u>drastic</u> — he goes from <u>bullying</u> Mickey in Act One to <u>killing</u> a petrol station attendant in Act Two.

2) When Sammy robs the bus conductor, an actor could use <u>physical gestures</u> such as a <u>clenched fist</u> or a <u>tapping foot</u> before he pulls out the knife — this would suggest that <u>rage</u> is slowly <u>building</u> inside him and he's about to do something <u>reckless</u>.

3) When he robs the filling station, an actor could use a <u>forceful tone</u> and a <u>higher pitch</u> when he says "Listen, it's not a toy, y' know" to suggest that Sammy is full of <u>adrenalin</u>. He could speak <u>breathlessly</u> and at a <u>fast pace</u> when he says "We're not playin' games" — this might suggest that Sammy is <u>panicking</u> and desperate to <u>get away</u>.

The actor on the left uses a confident stance and aggressive facial expressions.

© Donald Cooper/ photostage

> **Effect on the Audience**
>
> The more an actor emphasises Sammy's <u>panic</u> at this moment, the more it will seem like Sammy has created a situation he <u>can't control</u> — this <u>wouldn't redeem</u> Sammy's actions, but it would show he <u>isn't comfortable</u> with how far the situation has gone.

EXAM TIP

You've been struck by a smooth criminal — or not...

We can all agree that Sammy's bad news. For the exam, have a think about which physical and vocal performance skills an actor could use to get across his erratic and unpredictable nature to the audience.

Character Performance — The Narrator

You know that one person in your life who's just a bit of a know-it-all? That's basically the Narrator. This guy knows everything — and I mean everything — and spends the whole play showing off about it.

The Narrator acts as a storyteller

The Narrator also plays some of the minor characters — see p.39.

1) The Narrator helps to tell the story of *Blood Brothers* — he comments on what's happening in the play, observes the other characters and explains things to the audience.

2) He is detached from the play's main action and doesn't have relationships with any of the other characters — he doesn't react emotionally to what happens in the play.

> **The Narrator is...**
>
> **menacing**: "Did you forget about the reckoning day?"
>
> **mysterious**: "if only the three of them could stay like that for ever"
>
> **unsympathetic**: "did y' never hear of the mother, so cruel"

3) The Narrator has power over the story. During the montage in Act Two, when the scene freezes, the Narrator keeps talking — this shows that he has the ability to interrupt the action on stage.

4) He doesn't change or age during the play. His purpose and motivation remain the same — to tell a story.

5) Unlike the play's other characters, he doesn't belong to a particular social class. This marks him as an outsider and also helps to make him an impartial observer. He uses both standard and non-standard language so an actor might vary his accent throughout the play (see p.23 for more on his speech).

6) He is usually invisible to the other characters on stage, but he can sometimes be seen by them. For example, he takes a photograph of Mickey, Edward and Linda during the montage in Act Two.

He's sinister and menacing...

1) The Narrator constantly reminds the audience that Mickey and Edward are going to die — this gives him a threatening air.

2) An actor playing the Narrator could communicate this to the audience using a range of vocal skills:

- The Narrator's lack of emotion makes him seem sinister. An actor could use a matter-of-fact tone to say "did you never hear how the Johnstones died" to emphasise his coldness.

- He could move silently around the stage when other characters can't see him — this would make him seem ghostlike and mysterious.

- When the Narrator makes threats, an actor could use a low pitch and a menacing tone of voice to make him sound more sinister.

... and he's an imposing figure on stage

1) The Narrator has a strong presence on stage — he knows everything about the other characters and this makes him seem powerful.

2) A director might cast a tall actor with a strong build to make the Narrator seem more imposing, but an actor could also create this impression through his performance:

- He could use a straight posture to make himself seem taller, or draw back his shoulders and stand with his legs apart — this powerful stance would make him seem commanding.

- An actor could use controlled and confident movements to show the Narrator's power. Standing still would also make him look calm and give the impression that he is in control.

Character Performance — The Narrator

The Narrator highlights the characters' troubled consciences

1) The Narrator often explains the <u>thoughts</u> and <u>motivations</u> of characters when they're facing <u>serious decisions</u> — his dialogue reveals the '<u>conscience</u>' of these characters. This helps the audience to understand the <u>subtext</u> (the unspoken or hidden meaning) behind the characters' <u>speech</u> and <u>actions</u>.

2) For example, when Linda <u>phones</u> Edward in Act Two, the Narrator <u>reveals</u> her motivations to the audience — he explains that she wants to "get <u>free</u>" from her difficult life, but that betraying Mickey isn't an <u>easy decision</u> for her.

3) An actor could use <u>physical skills</u> to emphasise this aspect of the Narrator:

> **Effect on the Audience**
>
> The Narrator <u>encourages</u> the audience to "<u>judge</u>" who is at <u>fault</u> — revealing the characters' motivations gives the audience the <u>information</u> they need to do this.

- The Narrator could stand at Linda's <u>shoulder</u> and <u>pace</u> from one side to the other — this would visually represent her <u>inner conflict</u> as she tries to <u>choose</u> between Mickey and Edward.
- He could also <u>mirror</u> Linda's movements such as <u>walking</u> in the <u>same direction</u> and <u>turning</u> at the <u>same time</u> — this would highlight that he is acting as her <u>conscience</u>.

He plays lots of minor characters in the play

The Narrator plays a <u>variety</u> of <u>minor characters</u> who can be '<u>seen</u>' by the <u>other characters</u>. These roles require an actor to use a range of <u>vocal</u> and <u>physical skills</u>:

Vocal Skills

- An actor might use an <u>indifferent tone</u> for the Milkman and a <u>flippant tone</u> for the Gynaecologist to show that they are <u>uncaring</u>, as these characters emphasise that society is <u>unsympathetic</u> towards Mrs Johnstone's situation.
- An actor could use a prestigious accent like <u>Received Pronunciation</u> when he's playing Edward's Teacher and a <u>Liverpudlian accent</u> when he's playing Mickey's Teacher. Using <u>different accents</u> would highlight the <u>difference</u> in the Teachers' <u>social class</u> for the audience.

© David Cooper Photo

Physical Skills

- For the Conductor, an actor could use a <u>serious facial expression</u> and <u>intense eye contact</u> to seem <u>sinister</u> and create a <u>darker mood</u> on stage when he says "Happy are y'? Content at last?"
- When playing these minor roles, an actor might use <u>mannerisms</u> that the Narrator has used. This would show it is 'the <u>Narrator</u>' who is <u>playing</u> these characters, <u>not</u> the <u>actor</u> for the Narrator.

REVISION TASK

Haters gonna hate, narrators gonna narrate...

Find the Narrator's monologue in Act Two that begins "It was one day in October". Write a short paragraph about how you would make the Narrator seem ominous. You should consider:

1) The vocal skills you would use.
2) Your use of movements and gestures.
3) How you would use proxemics.

> Tick list:
> ✓ vocal skills
> ✓ physical performance
> ✓ proxemics

Character Performance — Other Characters

Linda's Mate, the Woman in Act One — *Blood Brothers* is full of fascinating and memorable characters. Okay, so some parts are bigger than others, but let's see how you might perform some of the minor roles...

Mr Lyons is a traditional middle-class father

1) Mr Lyons is the <u>breadwinner</u> in a conventional <u>nuclear family</u>. He has a <u>highly-paid job</u> and leaves <u>household</u> matters to his <u>wife</u> — he might <u>wave dismissively</u> as he says "The house is your domain" to show his <u>lack of interest</u>.

2) His main concern is his <u>business</u>. When he's around his <u>family</u>, an actor may seem <u>distracted</u> or <u>rush his lines</u> to suggest that he just wants to get back to <u>work</u>.

3) He <u>doesn't</u> have a <u>close relationship</u> with Mrs Lyons — he is <u>dismissive</u> of her <u>worries</u> about Edward and blames her "nerves". An actor could show their <u>cold relationship</u> through <u>proxemics</u> by putting <u>distance</u> between them on stage.

4) He represents <u>uncaring employers</u> — when he <u>fires</u> his workers in Act Two, an actor could use a <u>casual tone</u> and an <u>unconcerned facial expression</u> to make him seem <u>heartless</u>.

© David Cooper Photo

The Policeman in Act One reveals class prejudices

1) When Mickey and Edward get in <u>trouble</u> with the Policeman, he treats them very <u>differently</u> — he tells Mrs Johnstone it was a "serious crime" and tells Mr Lyons it was a "prank". His <u>attitude</u> represents the <u>prejudice</u> that the authorities had against the <u>working class</u> in the late 20th century.

2) An actor could use different <u>vocal tones</u> to highlight the Policeman's <u>different attitudes</u> towards the two families — he might use an <u>aggressive tone</u> as he tells Mrs Johnstone "there'll be no more bloody warnings" and a <u>polite tone</u> with Mr Lyons as he calls him "sir".

Character Performance — The Policeman

- Mr Lyons is <u>wealthy</u> and <u>middle class</u>, so the Policeman is reluctant to <u>use</u> his <u>authority</u> over him. An actor could use <u>movement</u> to show this.

- When he removes his <u>helmet</u>, he could <u>fidget</u> with it and pass it from <u>hand to hand</u> to show he isn't completely <u>at ease</u> around Mr Lyons.

- He could use <u>submissive body language</u> such as <u>bowing his head</u> when he takes the drink to show that he thinks Mr Lyons is <u>superior</u> to himself.

There are other characters who represent authority figures

1) The <u>debt collectors</u> in Act One represent the <u>different attitudes</u> that society might have towards Mrs Johnstone's situation. The Catalogue Man is <u>sympathetic</u> towards her — he could use an <u>apologetic facial expression</u> and an <u>awkward tone</u> as he says "I've got to do this, girl". In contrast, the Finance Man is <u>aggressive</u> — an actor could speak his lines <u>loudly</u> and lean <u>closer</u> to Mrs Johnstone.

2) The <u>Judge</u> is used to emphasise that Mrs Johnstone <u>disregards</u> the <u>seriousness</u> of Sammy's behaviour. An actor could use a <u>stern expression</u> and <u>confident gestures</u> when "*ticking Sammy off*" to show his <u>authority</u>. This would make it <u>funnier</u> for the audience when Mrs Johnstone "*bangs him on the head*".

Effect on the Audience

A director might have the <u>Narrator</u> play the Warder. This would highlight that the Narrator is <u>always watching</u> the other characters.

3) The <u>Warder</u> in Act Two <u>doesn't speak</u>, but he ushers Linda in and out of the <u>prison cell</u> — his silent presence enhances the <u>sombre atmosphere</u>. He could stand <u>motionless</u> while Linda and Mickey talk, using an <u>upright posture</u> and <u>crossing his arms</u> to create an <u>imposing presence</u> on stage.

Character Performance — Other Characters

Lots of the minor characters are stereotypes

1) Miss Jones represents people who became <u>unemployed</u> through <u>no fault</u> of their own. When Mr Lyons <u>fires</u> her, an actor could <u>keep writing</u> her *"notes"*, then <u>slowly stop</u> as she <u>realises</u> what has happened — this would show how <u>suddenly</u> she loses her job and make the audience feel <u>sympathy</u> for her.

2) Mrs Johnstone's daughter, Donna Marie, illustrates how easy it is for <u>working-class women</u> to get <u>trapped</u> in a life of <u>marriage</u> and <u>childbearing</u>. Her life follows the <u>same path</u> as Mrs Johnstone's — Mrs Johnstone says that her daughter is "A bit like me that way". An actor could use <u>similar mannerisms</u> to Mrs Johnstone to reinforce this resemblance.

3) Perkins is a <u>pupil</u> in Mickey's class — the Teacher's attitude towards him highlights the <u>poor opportunities</u> available to <u>working-class children</u>. He seems to <u>know</u> the <u>answer</u> to the Teacher's question, but the Teacher <u>ignores</u> him then <u>insults</u> him. An actor could hold his <u>hand up high</u> in the air to show that Perkins is <u>eager</u> to answer the question, and say "Sir, sir" with <u>more emphasis</u> each time to try to get the Teacher's attention.

An actor playing Miss Jones uses a distressed facial expression to show her shock.

© Australian Production 2015 / Produced by Enda Markey / Photograph by Kurt Sneddon

Character Performance — Minor Characters

- Actors could use <u>accents</u> to give <u>information</u> about undeveloped characters in the play — for example, Linda's Mate and the Woman who moves into the Lyonses' old house.
- Linda's Mate might have a <u>Liverpudlian accent</u> to suggest that she has a <u>similar background</u> to Linda.
- The Woman could use <u>Received Pronunciation</u> to suggest she is <u>middle class</u> like the Lyonses.

Some groups of characters have a particular purpose

The chorus might perform these groups of characters.

The minor characters in the play all have a <u>purpose</u> — for example, they might contribute to the <u>mood</u> of a scene or be used to send a <u>message</u> to the audience:

- The Kids in Act One bring <u>energy</u> to the stage. Actors could use <u>excited movements</u> and <u>high-pitched voices</u> when the <u>children play</u> to create a <u>lively</u> atmosphere on stage.
- The Neighbours' reactions provide <u>humour</u> when the Johnstones move away. Actors could <u>throw their hands up</u> in the air with joy to show how <u>relieved</u> they are that the Johnstones are leaving.
- The Dole-ites represent the <u>working-class men</u> who lost their jobs and had to live off <u>benefits</u>. Actors could use <u>slouched postures</u> and <u>gloomy facial expressions</u> to show how <u>dejected</u> they are.
- Edward's university friends show that his <u>new life</u> is drawing him away from Mickey. Actors could use a <u>prestigious accent</u> like Received Pronunciation to suggest they are <u>well off</u> and <u>upper class</u>.

REVISION TASK

I got my big break playing Neighbour No.3...

Imagine you're directing the scene in Act One where the Kids pretend to be gangsters. Write a paragraph explaining how the actors playing the Kids should perform their roles. You should:

1) Say where you would direct the actors to stand and how they should use the space on stage.
2) Describe how you'd direct the actors to interact with each other.
3) Explain the intended effect on the audience.

Tick list:
✓ blocking and stage space
✓ interaction with others
✓ effect on the audience

Practice Questions

After that section, you're probably bursting with brilliant ideas about how you could perform all the characters in the play. Thankfully, these practice questions are here to help you get those ideas down on paper...

Quick Questions

1) Give one reason why Mrs Johnstone struggles for money.

2) How might an actor use performance skills to show that Mrs Johnstone looks older than she is? Give one example.

3) Give one aspect of Mrs Lyons's backstory that explains the way she behaves in the play.

4) Find two quotes from the text that show that Mrs Lyons is manipulative.

5) What type of build might an actor playing Mickey have? Explain why.

6) How is Edward's upbringing different from Mickey's? Give three examples.

7) Give one example from the play where Linda shows loyalty.

8) How might an actor portray Sammy as intimidating in Act One?

9) What is the Narrator's purpose in the play?

10) Give two character traits that Mr Lyons shows in the play.

In-depth Questions

1) How might an actor playing Mrs Johnstone express her grief at the end of the play?

2) Explain how an actor might use performance skills to show that Mrs Lyons is more powerful than Mrs Johnstone in Act One.

3) How might an actor playing Mickey use performance skills to show that he is a child?

4) How does Linda change as she gets older? Explain how an actor might reflect this in their performance.

5) How might an actor playing Sammy show that he is out of control in Act Two?

6) Choose a moment from the play where the Narrator can't be seen by the other characters on stage. Explain how an actor playing the Narrator might interact with those characters.

Practice Questions

It's time for a few more exam style-questions. These are great for practising the longer answers that you might be asked to write in (you guessed it) the exam. To get the most out of these questions, don't just rattle through them as fast as you can — try to spend some time on each question and make sure you answer them properly.

Exam-style Questions — AQA

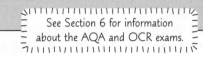

See Section 6 for information about the AQA and OCR exams.

> Find the part of Act Two where Linda and Mickey argue about his tablets. Read from "**Mickey *and* Linda *are in their new house.*"** to where Mickey says "**That's why I take them. So I can be invisible.**" Then answer Questions 1 and 2 below.

1) Imagine you're a performer playing Mickey. Describe how you would perform the line "**That's why I take them. So I can be invisible.**" using your vocal and physical skills. You should explain the effects you want to create.

2) Reread the last part of the extract, from "**Give them to me, Linda.**" to the final line.

   Imagine you're a performer playing Linda. Explain how you and the performer playing Mickey might use the space on stage and interact with each other to show the audience how Linda feels about him in this part of the extract.

> Read from the beginning of Act Two to where "***The Judge exits, stunned.***" Then answer Question 3.

3) Imagine you're a performer playing Mrs Johnstone. Discuss how you would use your performance skills to portray her in this extract. You should explain why your ideas are suitable for this extract and for the rest of the play.

Exam-style Questions — OCR

1) Explain how a performer might use stage directions to help them convey the character of Edward to the audience. Support your answer with examples from the text.

2) Imagine you're a performer playing the Narrator. Give three ways that you could use vocal skills to convey this character to the audience.

3) A director is staging the final moments of *Blood Brothers* when Mickey shoots Edward. How might they direct the performers during this part of the play to keep the audience engaged throughout?

Stage Types and Stage Design

The stage type and performance space need to work for the whole play, so a director needs to choose wisely...

'Blood Brothers' can be staged in different ways

1) *Blood Brothers* was <u>originally performed</u> on a <u>proscenium arch stage</u>, but a director can choose the stage type they think will <u>work best</u> for their own production. It's important to consider the <u>style</u> of the production when choosing a <u>stage type</u>:

> - A <u>naturalistic</u> production might use a stage type where the stage is <u>set back</u> from the <u>audience</u> — this helps maintain the 'fourth wall', which adds to the <u>illusion</u> that the audience is observing <u>real life</u> on stage.
> - A <u>non-naturalistic</u> production might use a stage type that brings the <u>actors</u> closer to the <u>audience</u>, making it <u>easier</u> for them to <u>break</u> the fourth wall.

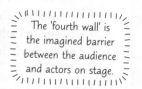
The 'fourth wall' is the imagined barrier between the audience and actors on stage.

2) Directors also need to think about the <u>practicalities</u> of the stage type they <u>choose</u>. For example, the audience's <u>line of sight</u> (their view of the action on stage) can be affected by the <u>type of staging</u> being used — directors need to make sure that the <u>impact</u> of <u>important moments</u>, such as Mickey's speech about <u>identity</u> at the end of the play, aren't <u>lost</u> as a result.

Different stage types create different effects

1) **Proscenium arch** and **end-on staging** allow directors to use <u>backdrops</u> and <u>large pieces of scenery</u> without <u>interrupting</u> the audience's <u>line of sight</u>. This is useful for a production of *Blood Brothers*, as Russell intended that the <u>sets</u> for the Johnstones' and the Lyonses' houses <u>remain on stage</u> throughout most of the play (see p.46).

This Broadway production was performed on a proscenium arch stage, so the director was able to use a large backdrop and an extensive lighting rig.

Effect on the Audience

> These stage types might make it <u>harder</u> for members of the <u>audience</u> to see the actor's <u>facial expressions</u>, which could <u>reduce</u> the <u>emotional impact</u> of the play.

2) **Thrust staging** can create a more <u>intimate</u> atmosphere because the actors are <u>closer</u> to the audience. Staging <u>key emotional moments</u> on the <u>apron</u> would give the audience a <u>clearer view</u> of the actors, so it would be easier for them to form an <u>emotional connection</u> with them.

3) **Traverse staging** positions audience members on <u>opposite</u> sides of the stage so they are <u>facing</u> one another. This staging would <u>remind</u> the audience that they are <u>observers</u> who are expected to "<u>judge</u>" the actions of the <u>characters</u> on stage and decide what is to <u>blame</u> for the tragic ending of the play.

4) **Theatre in the round** can create a very <u>intimate</u> and <u>intense</u> atmosphere, as the audience completely <u>surrounds</u> the actors. This might reinforce the idea that the characters are <u>unable to escape</u> their <u>fate</u>.

5) **Promenade theatre** helps the audience feel <u>more involved</u> in the play because they <u>move</u> with the actors to different settings. However, the <u>action</u> in *Blood Brothers* is meant to be <u>continuous</u> — this staging would <u>disrupt</u> the <u>flow</u> of the action, as it would be <u>difficult</u> to move to <u>new locations</u> quickly.

6) **Site-specific theatre** can <u>immerse</u> the audience in the play's <u>setting</u>, but it would be <u>hard</u> to select a <u>location</u> that would accurately reflect the <u>wide range</u> of <u>settings</u> in *Blood Brothers*.

7) **Black box staging** can draw the audience's <u>focus</u> to the <u>actors</u> if the performance space remains <u>simple</u>. However, there would be <u>limited</u> lighting and sound <u>equipment</u> to work with, so it would be <u>harder</u> to achieve the <u>lighting</u> and <u>sound effects</u> Russell uses to <u>enhance</u> the <u>impact</u> of the play on the audience.

Stage Types and Stage Design

Staging and performance space are linked

1) Using a small space would mean that the sets for the Lyonses and the Johnstones' houses would be close together. Having these sets side-by-side would encourage the audience to compare them, reinforcing the differences between the boys' upbringings.

2) A large performance space would make it easier to create clear lines of sight between actors and the audience. This would be useful when two moments take place at once, such as when Sammy convinces Mickey to rob the petrol station at the same time as Edward proposes to Linda in Act Two.

© Neil J Halin

3) A director should also consider how different areas of the stage might be used for effect. To help with this, directors often imagine the stage as being split up into nine areas. When the audience is on more than one side, directors pick one part of the stage as 'downstage' and use this as a reference for the other terms.

The director of this production was able to use a large performance space to separate Edward from Mickey and Linda when they see him on the hill in Act Two.

4) The location of characters on the stage helps to shape the relationship between the audience and the actors. The audience is likely to pay more attention to characters who are downstage.

5) In Act One, the stage layout could be used to encourage the audience to focus on Mrs Johnstone. The set for the Johnstones' house could be downstage left and the set for the Lyonses' house could be upstage right. If the audience can see Mrs Johnstone's run-down house clearly they might feel more sympathy for her.

Upstage Right (USR)	Upstage Centre (USC)	Upstage Left (USL)
Stage Right (SR)	Centre Stage (CS)	Stage Left (SL)
Downstage Right (DSR)	Downstage Centre (DSC)	Downstage Left (DSL)

AUDIENCE

Entrances and exits can have dramatic impact

1) In *Blood Brothers*, actors need to be able to enter and exit the stage quickly and smoothly. This is often achieved by lighting changes that place actors in shadow, allowing them to exit the stage unnoticed.

2) However, directors also need to consider how entrances and exits might be built into their stage design to create the dramatic effects that Russell intended. Russell doesn't describe the location or nature of entrances and exits in his stage directions, so directors have some creative freedom:

- At the start of the play, Mrs Johnstone "*enters with her back to the audience*", which creates a sense of anticipation in the audience. A trapdoor and stairs could be built into the stage floor so an actor could slowly ascend into view without facing the audience, creating a similar sense of suspense.

- At the start of 'Kids' Game' in Act One, "*The children rush on*" as Mrs Lyons exits. The actors could quickly access the stage using a series of walkways that run through the audience on to different parts of the stage — this would help to make their entrance feel sudden and chaotic.

3) Actors sometimes enter the performance space through parts of the set. In Act One, "*debt collectors emerge*" from Mrs Johnstone's house. The set for her house could be positioned next to the wings so the actors can access the back of the set without being seen by the audience and burst onto the stage.

Examiner enters stage right, to boos from the students...

When you're writing about staging, make sure you consider the effect that your stage design might have on the audience. Staging choices can have a major impact on how the audience experiences the play.

Set Design

Set designers have an important role — they need to consider how to create effective settings, convey themes and messages to the audience, and enhance the play's mood and atmosphere. No pressure there then...

'Blood Brothers' suits a composite set

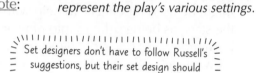
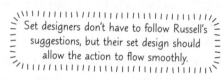

This production's composite set used elements of scenery to represent the play's various settings.

© Neil J Halin

1) The play is <u>set</u> in several <u>different locations</u> in Liverpool and Skelmersdale, including the <u>Johnstones' house</u>, the <u>Lyonses' house</u>, the <u>street</u>, the twins' <u>classrooms</u>, a <u>prison</u> and a <u>town hall</u>.

2) The <u>transitions</u> between these settings need to be <u>smooth</u> and <u>quick</u>, and some parts of the play use <u>more than one</u> setting <u>at once</u>. As a result, *Blood Brothers* is often staged using a <u>composite set</u> — where <u>several locations</u> are shown on stage at the same time.

3) Russell suggests a <u>basic layout</u> for the set in his <u>production note</u>:

> • There are two "<u>*semi-permanent*</u>" areas of the set — the <u>Lyonses' house</u> and the <u>Johnstones' house</u>.
> • All of the <u>other settings</u> are located on "<u>*communal ground*</u>" in the <u>space between</u> the two houses.

Set designers don't have to follow Russell's suggestions, but their set design should allow the action to flow smoothly.

4) The play was written to be performed with a <u>minimalist set</u> (with little scenery and few props), but Russell doesn't give <u>details</u> about what the settings should <u>look</u> like. Designers can choose <u>how</u> to represent the locations in the play, but they should consider the <u>overall aim</u> and <u>style</u> of the production:

> • <u>Naturalistic</u> set design can be used to create a <u>realistic</u> impression of Liverpool and Skelmersdale in the late 20th century. This would make the <u>settings</u> more <u>believable</u> for the audience.
> • <u>Minimalist</u> set design that includes elements of <u>symbolism</u> could be used to emphasise the play's <u>themes</u>. This would encourage the audience to focus on the play's <u>messages</u>.

Set design can help to establish setting

1) <u>Scenery</u> can be used to show <u>location</u>. For example, in Act One, a <u>cyclorama</u> with the image of a <u>cityscape</u> projected onto it could be used to represent <u>Liverpool</u>. At the end of the act, this image could be <u>replaced</u> by one showing <u>sweeping fields</u> to reflect the more <u>rural</u> setting of <u>Skelmersdale</u>.

2) In <u>naturalistic</u> set designs, <u>small details</u> can be used to make settings feel <u>authentic</u>. For example, the Johnstones live on a <u>terraced street</u> in an <u>industrial city</u> — a designer could use <u>flats</u> to create soot-blackened <u>brick walls</u> for the <u>exterior</u> of the house. The <u>front door</u> might be covered in <u>peeling paint</u> and the windows might be <u>cracked</u> to suggest that the area they live in is <u>run-down</u>.

Context — Housing

There was a <u>big difference</u> in the <u>quality</u> of housing that was available to <u>working-class</u> and <u>middle-class</u> people in Liverpool in the <u>1960s</u> (see p.7). A set designer can emphasise this by creating a <u>contrast</u> between the <u>condition</u> and <u>size</u> of the Johnstones' and Lyonses' houses.

3) In contrast, the Lyonses live in a <u>nicer area</u> in a "rather <u>large</u>" house near the <u>park</u>. The <u>set</u> for the Lyonses' house could have a <u>broader frontage</u> than the Johnstones' house to suggest that it is <u>much bigger</u>. A wide <u>bay window</u> and a <u>tall</u>, <u>shiny</u> front door with a <u>polished silver</u> door knocker could be used to make the house seem <u>grand</u>.

4) Set design can also indicate a certain <u>time period</u>. For example, the <u>interior</u> of the Lyonses' house in Act One might include a <u>patterned floral wallpaper</u> to reflect <u>fashions</u> of the <u>1960s</u>. After Mickey loses his job in Act Two, a <u>backdrop</u> with <u>graffiti</u> protesting against <u>redundancy</u> painted on it might be used near the Johnstones' house to suggest a <u>1970s setting</u> (see p.8).

Set Design

Details of set design can create symbolism...

1) Details of design, such as <u>colour</u> and <u>scale</u>, can be used to create <u>meaning</u> for the audience.

COLOUR

A designer might use <u>colour symbolism</u> (see p.51) to convey <u>messages</u> to the audience. For example, in Act Two, the Johnstones' front door could be <u>bright yellow</u> — this colour is associated with <u>happiness</u>, so it would symbolise their hopes for a <u>brighter future</u>.

SCALE

<u>Unrealistic scale</u> can be used to reinforce aspects of the play for the audience. Tall <u>trucks</u> with <u>oversized brick walls</u> painted on them could be positioned <u>upstage</u> and along both of the <u>wings</u>. This would emphasise that the characters are <u>trapped</u> and <u>can't escape</u> their fate.

2) <u>Non-naturalistic</u> productions of *Blood Brothers* are more likely to use elements of <u>symbolism</u>, because these productions <u>aren't</u> trying to reflect <u>real life</u>.

... and they can enhance atmosphere and mood

The tone of the play is darker in Act Two than in Act One (p.20) — set designers should consider how to enhance this shift in mood through their design.

1) The <u>overall mood</u> of *Blood Brothers* is <u>ominous</u> — a set designer could enhance this by using <u>cold colours</u> (such as blue and grey) throughout their design. This would create a <u>dark</u> and <u>unwelcoming atmosphere</u> on stage.

2) Designers also need to consider how to <u>reinforce</u> the <u>moods</u> that are created by <u>particular moments</u>:

MATERIALS

A <u>despondent</u> mood is created in Act Two when Mickey is put in <u>prison</u>. <u>Iron bars</u> could be lowered onto the stage to <u>surround</u> Mickey, emphasising the <u>harsh reality</u> of his situation and his <u>inability</u> to <u>escape</u>.

SHAPE

In Act One, a series of overlapping <u>triangles</u> with <u>sharp points</u> could be positioned upstage <u>above</u> the rest of the set to represent the <u>roofs</u> of terraced houses in Liverpool. These <u>jagged shapes</u> would look <u>chaotic</u>, enhancing the <u>unsettling atmosphere</u> of the play.

Levels can be practical and symbolic

1) <u>Rostra</u> (raised platforms) can be used to highlight <u>key moments</u> in the play. When Mickey <u>resists</u> taking his <u>pills</u> in Act Two while Edward and Linda are shown having an <u>affair</u>, he could stand on a <u>rostrum</u> at <u>centre stage</u> so that the audience can <u>clearly see</u> his struggle.

2) The <u>relationship</u> between <u>characters</u> can also be shown through <u>levels</u>. The Narrator could be positioned on a <u>higher level</u> than the other characters when he's <u>observing</u> them or <u>commenting</u> on their <u>actions</u>. This would <u>separate</u> him from the <u>main action</u>, emphasising his <u>status</u> as a <u>storyteller</u> who is <u>detached</u> from the other characters in the play.

3) Levels can be used to show characters' <u>status</u>. In Act One, the set for the Lyonses' house could be positioned on a <u>higher level</u> than the set for the Johnstones' house to symbolise the Lyonses' <u>superior social status</u>.

In this production, the Narrator observed the main action from a balcony in the set at various points in the play.

4) Levels can also be useful for showing <u>different settings</u> on stage at the same time. For example, during 'Long Sunday Afternoon', Edward could stand on a <u>separate level</u> to Mickey to show that he is in a <u>different location</u>. He could be positioned <u>directly above</u> Mickey to create the impression that the scene with Edward <u>only exists</u> *"in Mickey's mind"*.

Section Four — Staging and Design

Set Design

Technical devices can help the action flow smoothly...

1) <u>Technical devices</u> can be built into the set design to enable <u>rapid scene changes</u>. For example, in Act Two the <u>action</u> moves from the <u>street</u> to <u>Edward's school</u>. A <u>classroom</u> set could be mounted on <u>trucks</u> so that it can be <u>easily wheeled</u> onto the stage as the <u>previous scene</u> ends.

2) In Act Two, Mickey's <u>classroom</u> "*breaks up*" as the action moves to the scene where Mrs Lyons speaks to Edward about the locket. Any pieces of <u>scenery</u> used for the classroom could be attached to a <u>fly system</u> so they can be <u>quickly lifted</u> up off the stage to achieve this effect.

3) A <u>revolving stage</u> could be used to <u>enhance</u> the bus scene in Act Two — a 'bus' made out of <u>benches</u> could be positioned on a <u>revolving</u> part of the <u>stage floor</u> that surrounds the rest of the set. This would allow the bus to be <u>moved</u> to create the impression that it is <u>travelling</u>.

4) <u>Several locations</u> are shown in <u>quick succession</u> at the end of the play. A <u>projector</u> and a <u>backdrop</u> could be used to create a <u>sense</u> of these settings, instead of using <u>constructed scenery</u> that is <u>difficult</u> to <u>move</u>. For example, <u>prison bars</u> could be projected onto the backdrop to create a <u>prison cell</u>, and an ornate metal <u>railing</u> could be used to <u>signify</u> the <u>park</u> setting.

... and they can be used for dramatic effect

<u>Technical devices</u> can also be used to create <u>special effects</u> on stage.

1) <u>Smoke machines</u> could be used during the play's opening to release a <u>light mist</u> onto the stage. The Narrator could be <u>concealed</u> in the mist and then <u>move into view</u> when he "*steps forward*" to say his first line. This would make him seem <u>mysterious</u>, as well as adding to the <u>dreamlike atmosphere</u> of the play's opening.

2) <u>Pyrotechnics</u> could be used to create <u>loud bangs</u> and <u>sudden flashes</u> when Mickey shoots Edward and the police guns "<u>explode</u>" in Act Two. This would make the <u>gunshots</u> seem more <u>realistic</u>, which would make the <u>climax</u> of the play more <u>dramatic</u> and <u>intense</u> for the audience.

Smoke machines were used in this production to create an eerie atmosphere when Mickey and Edward become blood brothers.

© Eric Richmond / ArenaPAL

Explain the reasons for your design choices

It's important to <u>explain why</u> you'd design the set in a <u>certain way</u>. Here's an example:

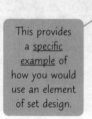

This provides a <u>specific example</u> of how you would use an element of set design.

___At the start of the play, I would use a printed backdrop of cracked___
brick walls to represent a terraced street in an impoverished area._____
As Mrs Johnstone sings "Once I had a husband", I would use a
flying rig to lower another printed backdrop behind her that shows a __
silhouette of a cityscape against a midnight blue sky with oversized, ___
glittery stars. This image would contrast with the run-down walls, ___
reinforcing that her youth was a better time for her, and it would _____
contribute to the dreamlike quality of her memories._____

This gives <u>precise details</u> about <u>colour</u> and <u>scale</u>.

This explains the <u>intended effect</u> on the <u>audience</u>.

Just don't put Sammy in charge of pyrotechnics...

EXAM TIP

The set doesn't just make the stage look interesting — it can really affect the audience's experience of the play. You need to explain what effect you'd want your design to have and how you'd plan to achieve it.

Props and Stage Furniture

Props and stage furniture help the audience understand details about the play's settings, themes and characters.

Props and stage furniture can help to establish setting...

1) *Blood Brothers* was written to be performed with the bare <u>minimum</u> of <u>props</u> and <u>stage furniture</u>. However, Russell mentions props and furniture that are important to the <u>plot</u> in his <u>stage directions</u>.

2) These objects can be used to give the audience <u>information</u> about a <u>setting</u>. For example, the props and furniture in the <u>Lyonses' house</u> in Act One could be used to highlight that it is a typical <u>middle-class household</u> — the "*armchair*" could be upholstered in an expensive <u>velvet material</u> to reflect their <u>wealth</u>, and the "*bookshelf*" could be stacked with heavy <u>hardback books</u> to reinforce that they are <u>well-educated</u>.

3) Single props or pieces of stage furniture can be used to <u>represent</u> a <u>setting</u>. For example, a <u>lamp post</u> could be placed on stage to suggest a <u>street</u> setting, and a short stretch of <u>wooden fencing</u> could be used to indicate a <u>garden</u> setting.

This production used a 1960s-style radio and pram to reflect the period when the play is set.

> **Staging**
>
> Using a simple piece of <u>stage furniture</u> to <u>signify</u> a <u>setting</u> instead of using an <u>elaborate set</u> would <u>speed up</u> scene changes, as it would be <u>easier</u> to move one object off the stage than it would be to move <u>constructed scenery</u>.

... and they can also create symbolism

See p.47 for more on symbolism in set design.

1) The <u>locket</u> that Mrs Johnstone gives to Edward symbolises the <u>connection</u> between Edward and the Johnstones. A prop designer might make this prop <u>oversized</u> to <u>draw</u> the audience's <u>attention</u> to this symbolism and reinforce the <u>natural bond</u> between the twins and Mrs Johnstone.

2) In the play, <u>guns</u> symbolise <u>loss of innocence</u>. In Act One, the children use harmless <u>toy guns</u> like Sammy's "*air pistol*", but in Act Two they use <u>real</u>, <u>deadly guns</u>. The design of these props could be used to <u>emphasise</u> this <u>progression</u> — the toy guns could be <u>wooden</u> and painted in <u>bright colours</u> to highlight that they're <u>fake</u>. In contrast, the gun Mickey uses to shoot Edward in Act Two could look <u>dark</u> and <u>metallic</u> so it seems more <u>realistic</u>.

Personal props can enhance characterisation

A <u>personal prop</u> is a prop that is used by an <u>actor</u> to add <u>depth</u> to their character:

- Props can be used to highlight a character's <u>status</u> or <u>occupation</u>. For example, in Act One, Mrs Johnstone carries "*a brush, dusters and a mop bucket*" when she enters the Lyonses' house — this <u>reveals</u> her <u>role</u> as the Lyonses' <u>cleaner</u> and reinforces her <u>working-class status</u> to the audience.
- They can also help to convey a character's <u>emotional state</u>. In Act Two, Linda is "*weighed down with shopping bags*" — these props emphasise the burden that she feels because of her <u>role</u> as a <u>mother</u> and <u>wife</u>. They might be designed to look <u>bulky</u> so it seems like she's carrying a <u>heavy load</u>.

Stage properties: flat, wooden, curtains on either side...

If you're writing about props and stage furniture in the exam, make sure that you can explain how details like the material, colour and size of these items can be used to convey certain messages to the audience.

Lighting

Lighting is really important when staging a production of *Blood Brothers* — after all, you don't want to leave your audience in the dark. Luckily for you, these pages about lighting design are really illuminating.

Lighting should support the style of a production

1) Russell includes some <u>stage directions</u> about lighting in the play. He occasionally suggests how lighting can be used to indicate <u>scene changes</u>, but he <u>doesn't</u> give specific <u>details</u> about how the lighting should <u>look</u>. This means that lighting designers have <u>freedom</u> when deciding which <u>lighting effects</u> to use.

2) *Blood Brothers* contains a <u>mix</u> of <u>naturalistic</u> and <u>non-naturalistic</u> elements (see p.19) so designers might use a <u>range</u> of lighting effects. However, these effects should match the <u>overall style</u> of the production.

3) In a <u>naturalistic production</u>, lighting effects should make settings seem <u>realistic</u>. A designer might mimic the effects of <u>real light sources</u> that would have appeared in the play's <u>settings</u>, such as <u>street lamps</u> or <u>electric lights</u>. This would help to make the settings more <u>convincing</u> for the audience.

4) In a <u>non-naturalistic production</u>, designers have more freedom because lighting <u>doesn't</u> have to create a realistic impression. This means they can use lighting in more <u>abstract</u> or <u>surreal</u> ways to create different <u>dramatic effects</u>.

This production used shadow and non-naturalistic purple lighting to create an ominous mood.

Setting can be established through lighting

1) Lighting can be used to suggest a <u>time of day</u>. During the montage in Act Two, a designer could use lighting with <u>cool tones</u>, such as blue or purple, to show that it's <u>night</u> when Mickey, Linda and Edward are *"coming out of the chip shop"*. Lighting with <u>warm tones</u>, like yellow and orange, can be used to suggest that it is <u>daytime</u> when they're at the beach.

2) It can also reinforce <u>location</u>. For example, after Mrs Lyons slaps Edward in Act One, the setting moves from <u>inside</u> their <u>house</u> to the <u>street</u>. Floodlights could be used to create a wash of <u>bright</u>, <u>yellow light</u> to suggest <u>sunshine</u>, indicating that the action has moved <u>outdoors</u>.

3) Lighting can also be used instead of scenery to show a <u>change</u> in <u>location</u>. For example, the Johnstones move from <u>Liverpool</u> to <u>Skelmersdale</u> at the end of Act One. This change happens during a song, so there's <u>no time</u> for a big <u>set change</u>. A lighting designer could use <u>gobos</u> to cast images of <u>trees</u> onto a <u>backdrop</u> to show the <u>shift in location</u> to rural Skelmersdale.

Lighting can support the action on stage

> In *Blood Brothers*, a new scene often begins on a different part of the stage from the previous scene. Lighting can be used to help the audience follow these changes.

1) As well as establishing setting, lighting is also essential for making sure that the audience can <u>see</u> what is <u>happening</u> on stage.

2) It can also be used to <u>direct</u> the audience's <u>attention</u> to specific parts of the stage:

- When Mr Lyons puts the <u>shoes</u> on the table in Act One, they could be lit with a <u>profile spotlight</u> to draw the audience's <u>attention</u> to them. This would make it <u>clearer</u> to the audience <u>what</u> Mrs Lyons is <u>reacting</u> to when she <u>suddenly stops speaking</u> and rushes towards the table.

- During 'Long Sunday Afternoon', *"The lights <u>fade on</u> Edward as the music shifts"*. When the lights *"fade"*, the <u>lanterns</u> that are positioned over <u>Edward</u> could be slowly <u>dimmed</u> until he's in <u>shadow</u>, bringing the audience's attention <u>back to Mickey</u> as he sings the final verse of the song.

Lighting

Lighting can be used symbolically

1) Lighting can be used to <u>represent</u> something else, such as a character's <u>emotions</u>. For example, when Mickey is in the prison cell in Act Two, the <u>intensity</u> of the lights around him could <u>lessen</u> gradually as he "*stands quietly crying*" — this <u>fading light</u> would symbolise his <u>loss of hope</u>.

2) <u>Colour symbolism</u> can be used to reinforce aspects of the play. For example, when Mickey confronts Edward at the end of Act Two, lights could be focused through <u>red gels</u> to create a <u>wash of red light</u> on stage. Red is associated with <u>danger</u> and <u>blood</u>, so this would <u>foreshadow</u> the bloodshed at the end of the play.

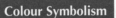

Symbolic lighting is more likely to be used in a non-naturalistic production.

3) <u>Shadow</u> can also be used symbolically. In Act One, Mrs Lyons <u>fires</u> Mrs Johnstone to keep her away from Edward. Lanterns lighting the area of stage between Mrs Johnstone and Edward's <u>cot</u> could be <u>dimmed</u> to create a <u>line of shadow</u> across the stage <u>between</u> them, symbolising their <u>separation</u>.

Colour Symbolism

Colour symbolism uses the <u>feelings</u> and <u>ideas</u> that are associated with certain <u>colours</u> to create <u>meaning</u> for the audience.

Lighting can reinforce mood and atmosphere

1) Lighting can be useful for <u>creating</u> a <u>threatening atmosphere</u> on stage. For example, after Mrs Lyons sweeps the shoes off the table when Edward is missing, lighting could be used to reflect her <u>fear</u> and create a <u>tense mood</u>:

© Eric Richmond / ArenaPAL

- The actor playing Mrs Lyons could be lit with <u>side lights</u> so her <u>face</u> is illuminated. This would make her <u>panicked</u> and <u>frightened</u> facial expressions more <u>visible</u> to the audience, highlighting her <u>fear</u>.

- <u>Downlighting</u> could be used to cast <u>strange shadows</u> on the <u>face</u> and <u>body</u> of the Narrator. This would make him seem <u>sinister</u>, creating a <u>threatening</u> atmosphere on stage that is <u>unsettling</u> for the audience.

2) When Mickey is arrested, <u>Fresnel spotlights</u> focused through <u>blue gels</u> could be used to cast sweeping beams of <u>blue light</u> over the stage to imitate the lights on a <u>police car</u>. The <u>slowly moving</u> light and <u>cool blue tones</u> would enhance the <u>tragic atmosphere</u> of the moment.

3) Lighting can also be used to enhance the <u>atmosphere</u> of a setting. In Act Two, when Mrs Johnstone sees Edward again, <u>birdies</u> with <u>orange</u> and <u>red</u> tinted <u>gels</u> attached could be concealed within <u>lampshades</u> hanging <u>above</u> the set for the <u>kitchen</u>. The <u>warm tones</u> of these lights would help to create a <u>homely</u> and <u>comfortable</u> atmosphere, making Mrs Johnstone's house seem <u>safe</u> and <u>welcoming</u>.

4) Changes in lighting can also be used to indicate a <u>shift</u> in <u>mood</u>. In Act Two, <u>Fresnels</u> could be used to create a <u>wash</u> of <u>soft lighting</u> on stage to reflect the <u>joyful mood</u> when Mickey and Linda get <u>married</u>. When Mickey goes to work "*only to have his cards given to him*" the mood becomes more <u>sombre</u>. The <u>intensity</u> of the lighting could <u>increase</u> until there is a wash of <u>bright</u>, <u>harsh light</u> on stage. This would reflect the shift to a more <u>serious</u> mood.

Special Effects

When Mickey is searching for Edward in Act Two, the <u>atmosphere</u> is <u>frantic</u>. Using <u>strobe lighting</u> at this moment would make the actor's movements seem <u>jerky</u> and <u>unnatural</u>. This would be unsettling for the audience and add to the <u>chaotic atmosphere</u> on stage.

Lighting

Lighting can support characterisation

1) Lighting can be used to emphasise the <u>qualities</u> of a particular character:

> • For example, when Mickey and Edward first meet as children, the stage could be lit with <u>floodlights</u> to create a <u>bright wash</u> of <u>white</u> light over them. White is associated with <u>goodness</u> and <u>innocence</u>, so this lighting would reinforce their <u>youthful</u> and <u>innocent</u> nature.
>
> • After Mrs Lyons finds out about the locket in Act Two, <u>uplighting</u> could be used on the Narrator to cast a <u>large shadow</u> behind him. This would make him seem more <u>sinister</u> and <u>threatening</u>.

This production trained several spotlights on the Narrator to cast shadows all around him.

2) The <u>relationship</u> between characters can be <u>reinforced</u> through lighting. When Linda and Edward meet at Christmas, a <u>Fresnel</u> with a <u>pink gel</u> could be used to cast <u>rose-tinted light</u> over them. Pink is associated with <u>love</u>, so it would show their <u>romantic feelings</u> for each other.

3) A character's <u>emotions</u> can be shown using lighting. When Mickey is released from prison, he is <u>sad</u> and <u>withdrawn</u>. A <u>bright side light</u> could be shone on his <u>upper body</u> to make his <u>face</u> more <u>visible</u> to the audience. This would emphasise the actor's <u>sad facial expression</u>, making his <u>depression</u> more <u>obvious</u>.

> **Special Effects**
>
> When Mickey is caught by the police in Act Two, a <u>gobo</u> attached to a <u>white profile spotlight</u> could be used to project vertical <u>prison bars</u> over the <u>body</u> of the actor who's playing Mickey. This would <u>symbolise</u> the <u>confinement</u> he faces and highlight that he is <u>trapped</u> in his situation.

Use technical terms when writing about lighting

When you're writing about lighting, it's important that you explain the <u>details</u> of your lighting design:

> Give <u>precise details</u> about the lighting equipment you'd use.

> When the children turn on Mickey during the game in Act One, I would train a bright profile spotlight on the actor playing Mickey and dim the lights over the rest of the characters. This would highlight his isolation from the others and emphasise that he is "*singled out*". When the children chant about hell, I would use lanterns with orange and yellow gels to introduce a fiery, sinister glow on stage. This would show the audience how threatened Mickey feels by their bullying.

> This explains the <u>reason</u> for the lighting choice.

> This gives the <u>intended effect</u> on the <u>audience</u>.

REVISION TASK — A nice bit of lighting can really brighten up your day...

Imagine you're a lighting designer for a production of 'Blood Brothers'. Write a paragraph about how you would light the ending of the play when Mickey confronts Edward. Write about:

1) The atmosphere you are trying to create.
2) Lighting effects you would use to do this.
3) How your choices might affect the audience.

> Tick list:
> ✓ dramatic intentions
> ✓ different types of lighting
> ✓ effect on the audience

Section Four — Staging and Design

Sound

Sound design is a noisy business (sorry, I couldn't resist). But seriously, sound has a key role in the play.

Sound designers should consider Russell's intentions

1) Russell gives information about <u>sound</u> in his <u>stage directions</u> for *Blood Brothers* — he indicates when <u>incidental music</u> and <u>songs</u> should begin and end, and he gives <u>descriptions</u> of <u>sound effects</u>.

2) Sound designers <u>don't</u> have to <u>follow</u> Russell's <u>instructions</u>, but they should consider the <u>dramatic effects</u> that he intended to create when making their <u>sound plot</u>. They should also make sure that their sound design is <u>in keeping</u> with the overall <u>style</u> of their production.

3) Designers should think about <u>how</u> Russell uses sound to:

- establish <u>setting</u>
- <u>support the action</u> on stage
- create or enhance <u>mood</u>
- show the <u>passage of time</u>
- create and maintain <u>tension</u>
- convey <u>meaning</u> to the audience

> A sound plot is a plan that contains a list of all the sounds and sound equipment used for a production. It also says when the sounds will be used.

Setting can be established through sound

1) Act One is set in a <u>residential area</u> of <u>Liverpool</u>. At the start of <u>outdoor</u> scenes, a sound designer could play a pre-recorded <u>soundscape</u> (a collection of sounds that are layered up to give a strong sense of place) featuring <u>children's voices</u>, <u>chattering residents</u> and a <u>bus</u> going past in the distance. This would help to establish the <u>urban street setting</u> for the audience.

2) When the Lyonses first arrive in <u>Skelmersdale</u> near the end of Act One, a <u>different soundscape</u> featuring farm animals <u>lowing</u>, birds <u>singing</u> and wind <u>rustling</u> through leaves could be played. This would <u>signify</u> to the audience that Skelmersdale is in a <u>rural</u> location.

3) Sound can also be used to show shifts in <u>time</u>. In Act Two, "<u>Christmas</u> bells" are used to show that there has been a <u>time jump</u> after Mickey gets <u>married</u> and <u>loses his job</u>.

Effect on the Audience

Blood Brothers is often staged with a <u>minimalist set</u> (see p.46), so it's not always <u>obvious</u> when the action has <u>moved</u> to a new <u>setting</u>. Directors can use sound to help the audience <u>follow</u> any changes in location.

Sound can reinforce actions

1) Sound can help to establish what is <u>happening</u> on the stage, e.g. a gunshot or a doorbell ringing. These sounds are often <u>diegetic</u> (sounds that <u>characters</u> can <u>hear</u>) and can be made <u>live</u> or <u>pre-recorded</u>.

2) <u>Offstage sound effects</u> can be used to show that <u>action</u> is happening <u>elsewhere</u>. For example, "<u>crying babies</u>" are heard <u>just after</u> Mrs Johnstone and Mrs Lyons make their <u>pact</u>. This tells the <u>audience</u> that the babies have been <u>born</u>. It's easier to <u>suggest</u> this through <u>sound effects</u> than it is to <u>show</u> their <u>birth</u>.

Effect on the Audience

<u>Offstage sound effects</u> are also usually <u>diegetic</u>. They can help to make the play more <u>believable</u>, as they make it seem as though the <u>events</u> on stage are taking place within a <u>wider world</u> that exists <u>beyond the stage</u>.

3) As well as conveying <u>actions</u> to the audience, sound can <u>enhance</u> the <u>impact</u> of an action. For example, a sound designer might play a <u>pre-recorded</u> sound of a <u>slap</u> when Mrs Lyons "<u>hits</u>" Edward. This would emphasise her <u>violent action</u>, making it seem even more <u>shocking</u> to the audience.

© Neil J Halin

Section Four — Staging and Design

Sound

Sound can add to mood and tension...

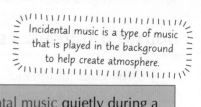

Incidental music is a type of music that is played in the background to help create atmosphere.

1) <u>Non-diegetic sounds</u> (sounds the <u>characters</u> on stage don't 'hear'), such as <u>incidental music</u>, can be used to create a certain <u>mood</u> or build <u>tension</u>:

- When Edward <u>moves</u> to Skelmersdale, <u>underscoring</u> (playing <u>incidental music</u> quietly during a scene) this moment with <u>slow</u>, <u>melancholy piano music</u> would reinforce the <u>sad mood</u> on stage.
- When Mrs Lyons <u>attacks</u> Mrs Johnstone in Act Two, each of her <u>violent movements</u> are "*punctuated*" by a single "*note*" — a sound designer could use <u>sudden bursts</u> of <u>low-pitched cello</u> music to draw attention to her <u>actions</u>, adding to the <u>tense atmosphere</u> of this moment.
- The <u>high-pitched sound</u> of a <u>violin</u> being played <u>rapidly</u> in a <u>minor key</u> could be used to create a <u>frantic atmosphere</u> when Mickey is searching for Edward in Act Two.

2) As well as <u>non-diegetic music</u>, sound designers can use <u>diegetic sound effects</u> to build <u>tension</u>. Before the <u>police</u> arrive at the end of the play, a <u>wailing siren</u> that gradually gets <u>louder</u> could be played to suggest that the police are getting <u>closer</u>. This would <u>build</u> the audience's <u>anticipation</u> of their arrival.

... and sound equipment can be used to enhance atmosphere

This production captured actors' voices using discreet earworn microphones, allowing the sound technician to control the volume of their voices.

1) A sound designer could use <u>sound equipment</u> to enhance the <u>actors' voices</u> to create a certain <u>mood</u>.

2) For example, in Act Two when the children <u>chant</u> "mad woman" at Mrs Lyons, a sound designer could <u>pre-record</u> the actors' voices and add <u>reverb</u> to create an <u>echo effect</u>. This would make their voices sound <u>eerie</u> and <u>unnatural</u>, which would add to the <u>unsettling atmosphere</u> of this moment.

Effect on the Audience

<u>Surround sound</u> could be used to <u>project</u> the children's voices sound <u>all around</u> the audience — this would <u>immerse</u> them in the sound of the chant, creating an even more <u>disturbing</u> and <u>intense</u> atmosphere.

3) When the Policemen <u>reassure</u> onlookers through a "*loudhailer*" after shooting Mickey at the end of the play, their <u>voices</u> could be captured by a <u>microphone</u> hanging <u>above</u> the stage and <u>amplified</u> so they are <u>unnaturally loud</u>. This would <u>bombard</u> the audience with their voices <u>immediately after</u> Mickey and Edward's <u>deaths</u>, creating a <u>chaotic</u> and <u>uncomfortable atmosphere</u>.

A sound designer might use sound to create symbolism

1) Sound can be used <u>symbolically</u> to convey <u>meaning</u> to the audience.

2) For example, a "*heartbeat*" is heard when Mrs Johnstone swears on the Bible, and it reaches "*maximum volume*" before the twins are <u>born</u>. This <u>increasingly intense</u> sound symbolises Mrs Johnstone's <u>inability</u> to <u>escape</u> the consequences of the pact. A sound designer might use <u>surround sound</u> to make the heartbeats <u>uncomfortably loud</u> and <u>overwhelming</u> for the audience so they feel <u>trapped</u> along with Mrs Johnstone.

3) When the <u>debt collectors</u> arrive to take <u>possessions</u> from Mrs Johnstone in Act One, a series of <u>slow</u>, <u>heavy knocks</u> could be used to announce their arrival. When Mrs Lyons arrives to <u>take Edward</u> later in the act, the <u>same</u> series of knocks could be played to symbolise that another <u>debt</u> is being <u>paid</u>.

Sound

Characterisation can be reinforced by sound

1) Productions of *Blood Brothers* normally create characterisation through the <u>actors' performances</u>, as well as their <u>costumes</u>. However, <u>sound</u> and sound <u>equipment</u> can be used to <u>add</u> to this characterisation.

2) For example, the <u>Narrator's voice</u> could be captured by a <u>wireless microphone</u> attached to his <u>costume</u> and routed through <u>speakers</u>. This would <u>amplify</u> his voice so that he sounds more <u>authoritative</u> and <u>commanding</u>, reflecting his <u>power</u> as a storyteller (see p.38).

3) <u>Incidental music</u> can convey <u>information</u> about a character. In Act Two when Mrs Lyons and Edward are "<u>waltzing</u>", a sound designer could <u>underscore</u> the scene with a piece of <u>classical piano music</u>. Classical music is <u>stereotypically</u> associated with the <u>middle class</u>, so this would <u>reinforce</u> their <u>social class</u> to the audience.

4) <u>Sound effects</u> can also be used to <u>aid</u> characterisation. For example, Sammy's <u>first entrance</u> in Act Two could be accompanied by a <u>faint police siren</u>. The audience would associate this sound with <u>criminality</u> and <u>danger</u>, so it would <u>hint</u> at his <u>lawless attitude</u>, as well as <u>foreshadowing</u> his criminal <u>behaviour</u> later in the act.

© Jeff Busby

Include specific details about sound in exam answers

If you're writing about sound, it's important to give <u>details</u> about <u>how</u> the sounds would be <u>made</u>:

This indicates what <u>sound equipment</u> would be used.

This gives <u>details</u> about <u>how</u> the sound would be <u>created</u>.

When the Narrator sings about the Devil pursuing Mrs Lyons after Edward goes missing in Act One, the song "ends with a percussion build to a sudden full stop". I would use a microphone to capture a live drum roll that has a rapidly building tempo. This would create an increasingly intense drumming sound that would enhance the unsettling atmosphere that is created by the Narrator's sinister lyrics about the Devil coming closer. I would use a single beat of a bass drum to create the "full stop", as this loud, booming sound would create a sense of finality before the sudden transition to the next scene.

This explains the <u>intended effect</u> on the audience.

REVISION TASK

My baby sister certainly doesn't need any amplification...

Create a sound plot for the montage in Act Two that shows Mickey, Linda and Edward's teenage years. Make a list of all the sounds that you might use. You should consider the following:

1) The sounds you would use, and whether they would be live or pre-recorded.

2) The style of your production and how this might affect your choices.

3) The effect the sounds might have on the audience.

Tick list:
✓ different sources of sound
✓ style of production
✓ effect on the audience

Section Four — Staging and Design

Costume

Whether your production is non-naturalistic or ~~naturist~~ naturalistic, the actors' costumes can convey a lot about them and the play. Time to summon your inner fashion designer, prepare the catwalk and read on...

Naturalistic costume design relies heavily on context

In a naturalistic production, costumes should reflect the play's context so they seem authentic. *Blood Brothers* is set between the 1950s and 1970s, and most of the action happens in the 1960s and 1970s. Designers need to consider the fashions of these decades when designing realistic costumes.

Materials

1) A variety of materials were used for clothing in the 1960s and 1970s — natural materials like wool, cotton and linen were common, and synthetic (man-made) materials like nylon and polyester were increasingly used.

2) Denim became popular in the 1970s — many people wore jeans and denim jackets. Leather jackets and leather trousers were also popular.

Condition

1) Between the 1950s and 1970s, lots of working-class people couldn't afford to buy new clothes regularly, so they often mended their clothes when they became worn out.

2) Middle-class people could afford to replace old clothing, so their clothes were more likely to look new and less likely to have visible patches or imperfections.

Style

1) Clothing styles became more varied in the 1960s, including hippie styles (colourful and gender neutral) and the Mod look (well-tailored).

2) However, many older adults still wore fashions that were popular in the 1950s. Women typically wore skirts or dresses with tights or stockings. Men often wore formal clothing such as straight trousers, suit jackets and a shirt and tie.

3) By the 1970s, many people wore more casual clothing such as jumpers, jeans and T-shirts with bright prints. It was also more common for women to wear trousers.

© Australian Production 2015 / Produced by Enda Markey / Photograph by Kurt Sneddon

Fit

1) Women's styles were quite modest in the early 1960s. Skirts and dresses were often flared and hemlines typically fell below the knee.

2) In the late 1960s, mini-skirts became popular amongst young people. Skirts were less flared and became more tight-fitting around the legs.

Colour

1) Bright colours were popular in the 1960s and 1970s, in contrast to the more conservative styles of earlier decades.

2) However, some items of clothing remained traditional, e.g. men's formal suits were usually black or grey.

Costumes can be non-naturalistic too

> It's important to consider the practical aspects of costume design — an actor should be able to move easily on stage and might need to make quick costume changes.

1) In a non-naturalistic production, costumes don't have to reflect the play's context. This means a designer can be more creative, but they still need to consider the effects their choices will have on the audience.

2) Non-naturalistic costumes might be used symbolically — a costume might represent important aspects of a character or highlight one of the play's themes.

3) For example, the Narrator might be dressed in present day fashions, such as a plain black T-shirt and slim-fit trousers, to contrast with the 20th-century clothes of the rest of the characters. This would make the Narrator stand out, highlighting that he is separate from the main action of the play.

Costume

Costumes can reveal basic information about a character...

1) Costumes can highlight a character's <u>age</u> — for example, Mickey's <u>clothes</u> can help to convey that he <u>ages</u> from a child to an adult. In Act One, he might wear <u>shorts</u> to emphasise his <u>youth</u>. At the start of Act Two, he might wear <u>full-length</u> trousers to show that he is <u>older</u>, or <u>jeans</u> to show that he has become more interested in <u>fashion</u> as a teenager.

2) Characters' <u>occupations</u> can be shown through their costumes. Mrs Johnstone might wear an <u>apron</u> to show that she works as a <u>cleaner</u>, while Miss Jones might wear a <u>smart blouse</u> and <u>skirt</u> to convey that she works as a <u>receptionist</u> in an office.

3) Costume can also show a character's <u>status</u> — at the end of the play, Edward could wear a <u>formal suit and tie</u> to emphasise he is a <u>politician</u>. Mrs Lyons might wear <u>expensive jewellery</u> to highlight that she is <u>wealthy</u> and <u>middle class</u>.

In this production, Mickey wears shorts and trainers to make him look more like a child.

Hair and Make-up

The <u>stage directions</u> say that Mrs Johnstone *"is aged thirty but <u>looks more like fifty</u>"*. A costume designer could make an actor look <u>older</u> by using hair chalk to add <u>streaks of grey</u> in her hair and a dark powder or eyeliner to add <u>lines</u> to her face. This would encourage the audience to feel <u>sympathy</u> for Mrs Johnstone — it would highlight the <u>difficult life</u> she has led and the <u>strain</u> she is under.

... and show aspects of their personality

1) A costume designer might dress Mrs Lyons in a <u>formal silk blouse</u> and <u>smart pencil skirt</u>, and her hair might be <u>styled neatly</u>. This would suggest that she cares about her <u>appearance</u> and how others see her.

2) In Act One, Mickey might have <u>messy hair</u> and be covered in <u>dirt</u> to show that he enjoys <u>playing outside</u>. In contrast, Edward might have <u>neat hair</u> and <u>clean clothes</u> to show he is <u>less adventurous</u> than Mickey.

3) Sammy might be dressed in <u>dark colours</u> throughout the play to reflect his <u>menacing</u> and <u>rebellious</u> nature.

4) Mr Lyons might be dressed in a <u>business suit</u>, even when he is at <u>home</u> with his family. This would convey to the audience that he is <u>preoccupied with work</u>.

> Colour can be used symbolically to convey meaning to the audience (see p.51). For example, black can be associated with mystery and power.

Costumes can have a symbolic meaning

1) Designers can use aspects of costume to <u>symbolise</u> something about a character for the audience.

2) At the end of Act Two, Mrs Johnstone could be wearing a <u>long</u>, <u>black coat</u> over her dress that falls below her knees. When the twins die, she could draw the coat around her body to <u>cover</u> the rest of her costume. This would symbolise her <u>grief</u> and the <u>impact</u> that her sons' <u>deaths</u> have had on her.

3) In Act Two, Mickey is dressed in "*working clothes*" at his wedding. A designer could dress Mickey in <u>factory overalls</u> throughout the rest of the act to symbolise that he <u>can't break free</u> from his <u>working-class identity</u>.

4) In a non-naturalistic production, the twins could be dressed in <u>white T-shirts</u> throughout the play. These shirts could each have a <u>jagged hole</u> the size of a <u>bullet</u> surrounded by a dark red stain to <u>symbolise</u> Mickey and Edward's inability to escape their violent <u>deaths</u>.

Effect on the Audience

This would make the scenes where the twins are children more <u>emotional</u> for the audience to watch, as it would <u>remind</u> them that the twins' happiness and innocence <u>won't last</u>.

Costume

Costume can be used to support the play's action

A director can use costume to help make the action on stage <u>clearer</u> for the audience:

- In Act Two, Sammy is seen *"pulling on a jacket"* as he <u>leaves the house</u>. This helps to reinforce that he is going <u>outside</u> as the scene <u>moves</u> from the Johnstones' <u>house</u> to the bus stop in the <u>street</u>.
- At the wedding, Mrs Johnstone *"<u>whips off her overalls</u> and a wedding suit is underneath"*. This shows the <u>quick scene transition</u> from Mrs Johnstone's <u>house</u> to Mickey and Linda's <u>wedding</u>.
- When Edward goes missing in Act One, Mrs Lyons's <u>hair and make-up</u> could highlight her <u>distress</u>. She could have <u>smudged mascara</u> around her eyes as though she's been <u>crying</u>, and her hair could also be <u>messy and tangled</u> to suggest that she has been running her hands through it in <u>despair</u>.

Changes in costume can reflect a change in character

1) In Act One, Mrs Johnstone might wear her hair in a <u>messy bun</u> to suggest that she is too <u>tired</u> and <u>stressed</u> to think about her appearance. At the start of Act Two, she is <u>happier</u> and has <u>fewer responsibilities</u> because most of her children have "flown the nest". Her <u>hairstyle</u> might <u>change</u> to reflect this — she could wear her hair <u>loose</u> and <u>flowing</u> to make her seem <u>carefree</u>.

2) Linda is <u>cheerful</u> as a teenager but grows more <u>tired</u> and <u>strained</u> after she becomes a wife and mother:

© David Cooper Photo

- She might wear a <u>short skirt</u> and <u>bright colours</u> at the beginning of Act Two to show that she is <u>young</u> and <u>enjoying</u> her life. As she gets older, her costume might change to show that she is <u>unhappy</u> — for example, she might <u>cover</u> her bright clothes with a <u>grey jumper</u>.
- When Linda has an affair with Edward, she feels <u>free</u> from her unhappy life with Mickey. This could also be reflected in her costume — she might wear a <u>dress</u> made from a <u>light</u>, <u>flowing</u> material.

In this production, Linda puts a baggy cardigan over the floral dress she wore as a teenager.

In the exam, think about what costume can tell the audience

When you're writing about costume in the exam, it's important to include lots of <u>details</u> about how the costume would <u>look</u>. Here's an example of how you might do it:

> In Act Two, I would dress Mickey in a school uniform of a white shirt, black polyester trousers and a tie to show that he is a pupil at a comprehensive school in the 1970s. The tie could be worn loosely fastened and at a short length, and his hair would be ruffled and messy. This would illustrate his rebellious personality and suggest to the audience that he doesn't take education seriously.

This gives <u>details</u> about <u>how</u> the costume would be <u>worn</u>.

This <u>explains</u> the choice of costume.

This explains the <u>effect</u> on the <u>audience</u>.

EXAM TIP

I tried to thread a costume joke together but didn't get far...

Clothing is an important part of costume design, but it isn't the only aspect — in the exam, make sure you think about hair and make-up as well and how you would use them to achieve the effect that you want.

Puppet Design

Puppets aren't normally used in productions of *Blood Brothers*, but they can help to bring the play to life.

Puppets should convey meaning

Puppet design is only an option on the AQA exam. If you're doing a different exam board, you don't need to read this page.

A <u>non-naturalistic</u> production may use puppets during <u>key moments</u>, or they might be used to perform the <u>entire play</u>. It's the <u>responsibility</u> of a <u>puppet designer</u> to think about how puppets can <u>communicate meaning</u> to the audience. There are some key <u>design elements</u> they should consider.

1) <u>Size</u> — If puppets are being used to represent <u>characters</u>, the puppets for Mickey, Edward and Linda could be <u>larger</u> in Act Two than in Act One to reinforce the idea that the characters have <u>grown up</u>.

2) <u>Colour</u> — Colour can be used <u>symbolically</u>. For example, a puppet that represents Edward in Act One could be made from <u>brightly coloured material</u> to reflect his <u>cheerful</u> nature.

3) <u>Material</u> — Puppet designers should consider the <u>texture</u> and <u>condition</u> of the materials they use. For example, a puppet representing Mickey could be made from <u>patchy</u> material that has a <u>coarse texture</u> to highlight his <u>poverty</u>.

4) <u>Shape</u> — A puppet representing Mrs Lyons in Act One might have <u>sharp</u>, <u>jagged</u> edges to hint that she is <u>dangerous</u> and not as <u>compassionate</u> as she appears.

Puppet Costumes

A puppet that represents a character may have a <u>costume</u>. The design of this costume could help to <u>characterise</u> the person that the puppet represents.

Puppets can enhance the action for the audience

Puppets can be used <u>alongside actors</u> to help the audience to <u>interpret</u> the action. For example, they might highlight an important <u>moment</u>.

SHADOW PUPPETS

- A designer could use <u>shadow puppets</u> behind a <u>gauze screen</u> to create <u>silhouettes</u> of dancing couples when Mrs Johnstone describes meeting her <u>husband</u> in Act One. This would give the impression of a <u>flashback</u> and reinforce that her dancing days are a <u>distant memory</u>.

- A shadow puppet could be used to create an <u>oversized silhouette</u> of the Devil behind an <u>actor</u> who is playing Mrs Johnstone when the Narrator says the "devil's got your number" for the first time. This <u>looming shadow</u> would emphasise that Mrs Johnstone <u>can't escape</u> her fate.

When Mrs Johnstone explains how she met her husband, this production included performers who acted out her story.

© David Cooper Photo

ROD PUPPETS

- In Act Two during the song 'Miss Jones', an actor playing <u>Mr Lyons</u> could <u>control</u> a rod puppet of <u>Miss Jones</u>. This would emphasise the <u>power</u> that he holds over her and reinforce the idea that her <u>fate</u> is in his hands.

STRING PUPPETS

- After Mrs Lyons exits Mrs Johnstone's kitchen in Act Two, <u>string puppets</u> of children could be <u>dropped down</u> around Mrs Lyons. They could be <u>moved jerkily</u> in time to the offstage "*chanting*" of "mad woman". This would illustrate Mrs Lyons's <u>mental breakdown</u>.

EXAM TIP

Marionette? But I thought Mickey married Linda...

Don't get your strings in a tangle about puppets — they're nothing to worry about. If you are writing about puppet design in the exam, make sure you explain how your design ideas will affect the audience.

Practice Questions

*That was a lot of information to take in, so have a go at these practice questions to check how much you've
learnt. If you're a bit wobbly about some of the answers, flick back through the section to refresh your memory.*

Quick Questions

1) Give two considerations that directors must make when
   choosing a stage type for a production of *Blood Brothers*.

2) Why might a set designer include levels in sets for the play? Give two reasons.

3) Give two ways that technical devices can be used
   to create dramatic effects in *Blood Brothers*.

4) How can personal props be used to reinforce characterisation? Give two examples.

5) Give two examples of how lighting might be used in a naturalistic production of the play.

6) What is diegetic sound?

7) How might incidental music be used to create tension? Give one example.

8) How might a costume designer use the condition of costumes
   to create meaning for the audience? Give one example.

9) Give one example of how a designer might use a character's costume to create symbolism.

In-depth Questions

1) Choose a stage type and explain the advantages and disadvantages
   of using it to stage a production of *Blood Brothers*.

2) Explain how you would design a set for Mickey and Linda's house in a naturalistic
   production of the play. You should refer to the play's context in your answer.

3) What props and stage furniture might a designer create for the montage in Act Two?
   Use examples from the play to back up your ideas.

4) What offstage sound effects would you use when the Johnstones move to Skelmersdale
   at the end of Act One? Explain how you would create these sounds.

5) How might a lighting designer use colour symbolism in a non-naturalistic production when
   Mrs Johnstone meets the Conductor in Act Two? Explain why your ideas are appropriate.

6) How might a costume designer dress Mrs Lyons to show that she's a middle-class character?

Practice Questions

Now that you're an expert on staging and design, it's time for a few more exam-style questions. Have a go at writing your answers in exam conditions, or get comfy with a cuppa and a biscuit. Whichever works for you.

Exam-style Questions — AQA

AQA and OCR questions are different — see Section Six for more.

> Find the part of Act One where Mickey tries to visit Edward after he has moved house. Read from "**Mickey *wanders away*"** to where Mickey says **"On this long, long, long / Sunday afternoon."** Then answer Question 1.

1) Imagine you're a lighting designer working on *Blood Brothers*. Describe how you would use lighting to create effects that reinforce the action in this extract. You should explain why your ideas are suitable for this extract and for the rest of the play.

> Find the part of Act Two where Edward's teacher confronts him about the locket. Read from where the Teacher says "**You're doing very well here, aren't you, Lyons?**" to where Edward exits. Then answer Question 2.

2) Imagine you're a set designer for a production of *Blood Brothers*. Explain how you would use staging and set design to portray this extract effectively on stage to the audience. You should refer to the play's context in your answer.

> Find the part of Act Two where Mickey is searching for Edward after learning about his affair with Linda. Read from "***As the music abruptly segues*"** to "***On the last 'Today' the music stops abruptly.*"** Then answer Question 3.

3) Imagine you're a sound designer staging this extract of *Blood Brothers*. Explain how you would use sound design to create effects that reinforce the action in this extract. You should explain why your ideas are suitable for this extract and for the rest of the play.

Exam-style Questions — OCR

1) Explain how a sound designer might use sound effects to enhance the action for the audience when Mickey and Sammy rob the filling station in Act Two. Support your answer with examples from the text.

2) Write a comparison of the advantages and disadvantages that a set designer might face if they were presenting *Blood Brothers* in the round.

3) Describe a costume for Linda and explain why your choices are suitable.

Act One

This section looks at performance skills and design features using the kind of close analysis you should be doing in the exam — how lovely. If you fancy a reminder of the plot, take a look at the introduction (p.4-5).

Act One creates contrasting moods

1) Act One plays a key role in setting the mood and atmosphere of the play — the mood of Act One is generally light-hearted, but there are also some serious moments that introduce a darker atmosphere.

2) There is an ominous atmosphere when Mrs Johnstone swears on the Bible that she will give one of the twins to Mrs Lyons. The Narrator's insistence that "there's no going back" suggests to the audience that their pact will have inescapable consequences, which foreshadows the twins' inevitable deaths.

© Jeff Busby

3) Mickey and Edward's interactions when they meet for the first time create humour and lighten the mood of the play. However, this lighter mood is briefly interrupted by a more serious moment when the boys make their own pact and become blood brothers.

4) One of the darkest moments in the act occurs when Mrs Lyons hits Edward. This is an unsettling moment for the audience — Mrs Lyons's aggressive reaction hints at her instability and foreshadows her violent behaviour in Act Two.

5) The light-hearted mood returns when Mickey, Edward and Linda play with Sammy's air pistol and are caught misbehaving by the policeman. This moment creates comedy for the audience as the children try to prove to each other that they aren't scared to throw stones at the window.

6) The end of Act One creates an optimistic atmosphere as the Johnstones learn that they're moving away — Mrs Johnstone is delighted and hopes that her family will have a fresh start. However, the audience questions whether things really will be different for the Johnstones in Skelmersdale.

Mrs Johnstone and Mrs Lyons make the pact

1) Mrs Lyons manipulates Mrs Johnstone into making the pact. An actor can use physical skills to emphasise her control and dominance over Mrs Johnstone.

2) When she says "we must make this a, erm, a binding agreement", she might use an upright posture to suggest that Mrs Lyons is trying to come across as authoritative and commanding.

> **Effect on the Audience**
>
> The more an actor emphasises Mrs Lyons's forcefulness, the more it will seem as though Mrs Johnstone had no choice and was pressured into giving Edward away.

3) She could use determined movements when she "shows the Bible to Mrs Johnstone" — she might hold the book out in front of her expectantly and nudge it towards Mrs Johnstone to pressure her into taking it. Her actions could then become more forceful — she might put her hand over Mrs Johnstone's and push it onto the bible, forcing her to make the pact. This would show that Mrs Lyons is in control.

Design — Lighting

- There is an ominous mood when Mrs Lyons suggests making the pact a "binding agreement". Lighting could be used to reinforce this. For example, uplighting could be used to cast shadows over Mrs Lyons's and Mrs Johnstone's faces as they swear on the Bible, creating an unsettling atmosphere.

- A barndoor could be used to create an area of shadow where the Narrator is standing so the audience can only hear his voice. This would enhance the sinister mood when he says "the thing was done".

- Light from Fresnels could be focused through a red gel to create a red wash on the stage. Red is associated with danger, so this colour symbolism (see p.51) would foreshadow the pact's tragic results.

Act One

Edward and Mickey become blood brothers

1) When Mickey and Edward make their pact, the atmosphere on stage becomes more serious. A sound designer might use music to enhance this shift in tone.

2) A long, low-pitched note of incidental cello music could be introduced when Mickey brings out the penknife. This would signify that something important is about to happen and increase the intensity of this moment for the audience. As the twins make their pact, the music could slowly increase in volume to reinforce the significance of this moment.

3) A designer could re-use the pattern of bass notes that they used to create the heartbeat sound effect when Mrs Lyons and Mrs Johnstone made their pact. This would symbolise how the mothers' actions have affected their sons' lives.

4) The music could stop abruptly when Sammy "leaps in front of them". This would make his interruption seem more sudden and clearly mark the transition away from this more serious moment in the play.

Physical Skills — Proxemics

- When the twins meet, they quickly form a connection — this could be shown using proxemics.
- An actor playing Edward could stand close to Mickey after he approaches him for the first time — this close proximity would show Edward's determination to make friends with him.
- Mickey might move away to increase the space between him and Edward — this would show his lack of trust. However, when Edward offers the sweets, Mickey could move closer to take one — this return to close proximity would suggest that Mickey's trust in Edward is growing.
- The twins "clamp hands together" when they make the pact. The actors could move together so that their faces are almost touching. This would emphasise the strength of their bond.

Mrs Lyons forbids Edward to see Mickey

© David Cooper Photo

1) Mrs Lyons panics when she realises Edward and Mickey have met — an actor could use vocal skills to show her emotional turmoil when she questions Edward about his friendship with Mickey.

2) An actor could use a fast pace and rising intonation as she asks Edward "where did you meet that boy?" This would suggest that she's desperate to discover the truth, which would highlight her panic and anxiety.

3) She might use a high pitch when she says "Edward, Edward, don't" to make Mrs Lyons sound upset and show she is "almost crying". When she says "It's only because I love you", she might return to a regular pitch to make her tone more gentle as she tries to persuade him that she is doing the right thing for him.

4) After Edward swears at her, she could increase the volume of her voice to show her anger. She could also speak more forcefully, placing emphasis on words such as "filth" and "horrible". Her voice could trail away as she says "you won't ever..." to show that she has noticed Edward's "terror".

Effect on the Audience

The sudden change in Mrs Lyons's behaviour is unsettling for the audience. It introduces a sense of danger, shifting the tone on stage.

5) When she cradles Edward, she could almost whisper the words "my son" and use a soft tone of voice. This would suggest to the audience that she is trying to make up for her anger and prove to herself that she is a good mother.

Act One

Mickey, Linda and Edward get into trouble

1) An actor could use <u>vocal skills</u> to show Mickey's <u>change in attitude</u> when he and Linda talk about <u>throwing stones</u> through the window.

2) Mickey might use a <u>goading</u> tone as he says "Ooh, I dare y', Linda" — this would show that he feels <u>confident</u> and wants to cause <u>mischief</u>.

3) He could use a <u>loud volume</u> and a <u>forceful tone</u> when he says "No he isn't!" — this would show that he is <u>defending</u> Edward. He could then return to a <u>goading tone</u> when he says "Are y', Eddie?" to suggest that he's trying to <u>encourage</u> Edward.

4) When the policeman catches them, an actor could show Mickey's <u>fear</u> by using a <u>high pitch</u> when he says "Sir." This would make him sound <u>nervous</u>, which would suggest that he feels <u>intimidated</u>.

Sound Design — Sound Effects

- The "<u>*metallic ping*</u>" of the air pistol could be created live offstage by throwing <u>pennies</u> at a sheet of <u>metal</u> and using a <u>microphone</u> to capture the sound. <u>Amplifying</u> this sound would draw the audience's attention to the <u>gunshots</u> and create a sense of <u>danger</u>.

- A <u>pre-recorded gunshot</u> might be used for the final shot to introduce an <u>atmosphere</u> of <u>danger</u> and <u>foreshadow</u> the use of real guns later in the play. <u>Reverb</u> could be added so the shot <u>echoes</u> around the theatre, increasing its impact on the audience.

The Johnstones learn that they're moving

1) The <u>mood</u> changes at the end of Act One when Mrs Johnstone gets a <u>letter</u> telling her she's <u>moving</u> to Skelmersdale. Mrs Johnstone is <u>overjoyed</u> and Act One ends on a <u>happy</u> and <u>hopeful</u> note. A prop designer might use this opportunity to emphasise that the Johnstones are escaping to a <u>better life</u>.

2) In a <u>non-naturalistic</u> production, the letter might be <u>golden</u> and <u>glittery</u> to <u>symbolise</u> that it is the Johnstones' '<u>golden ticket</u>' to a better life.

3) To emphasise the <u>poor condition</u> of the "*battered suitcases*", a designer could rub them with <u>sandpaper</u> to make them look <u>scuffed</u> and <u>faded</u>. They might also poke <u>holes</u> in the material to make the suitcases seem <u>old</u> and <u>damaged</u>. This would reflect the family's <u>poverty</u>.

4) Some of the "*rags*" could <u>already</u> be in the suitcases and <u>spilling out</u> messily to suggest that the family are <u>packing quickly</u> — this would show how <u>eager</u> they are to <u>leave</u> Liverpool for Skelmersdale.

5) Mrs Johnstone jokes that the <u>Pope</u> might come for tea — this emphasises her <u>high hopes</u> for the future. The picture of the Pope could be <u>oversized</u> so that the Pope is <u>recognisable</u> to the <u>audience</u> and to make this moment more <u>humorous</u>.

© Donald Cooper/ photostage

Physical Skills — Gestures and Movement

- An actor playing Mrs Johnstone could use <u>animated gestures</u> to show how she feels about moving. She might <u>throw her hands in the air</u> as if she's bursting with <u>joy</u>. This would be more effective if she used <u>slower</u> movements in <u>previous scenes</u>, as this contrast would highlight her <u>change</u> in <u>mood</u>.

- Mrs Johnstone could use <u>energetic</u> movements such as <u>skipping</u> and <u>jumping</u> to show how <u>excited</u> she is. This would <u>increase</u> the <u>pace</u> of the action and enhance the atmosphere of <u>optimism</u>.

Props to Mrs J — you've got to admire her optimism...

From the colour of a costume to subtle facial expressions — it's all done for a reason. Even the smallest details can affect the audience's overall experience of the play, so try to include them in your answers.

Act Two — Part One

In the first part of Act Two, the audience sees Mickey and Edward growing up and facing all the usual teen troubles — spots, school, romance, being reunited with your secret twin brother... Let's take a closer look.

The first part of Act Two develops key relationships

1) Act Two begins <u>seven years</u> after the end of Act One. The first part of the act establishes how the <u>characters</u> and their <u>relationships</u> have <u>changed</u> in that time.

© David Cooper Photo

2) Mickey and Linda are now <u>teenagers</u>, and their <u>friendship</u> has become <u>more complicated</u> — she <u>flirts</u> with him on their walk up the hill, but he feels too <u>awkward</u> to act on his <u>feelings</u> for her.

3) Mrs Johnstone is <u>shocked</u> when she meets Edward again. This moment highlights the <u>bond</u> between them — even though it's <u>years</u> since they've <u>seen</u> each other, she still <u>cares</u> about him and he still wears the <u>locket</u> that she gave him.

4) The <u>conflict</u> between Mrs Lyons and Mrs Johnstone reaches a <u>dramatic climax</u> when Mrs Lyons <u>attacks</u> Mrs Johnstone. This is a <u>shocking</u> moment for the audience that emphasises how <u>unstable</u> Mrs Lyons has become.

Mickey and Linda see Edward's house from the hill

1) Linda is <u>open</u> about her <u>attraction</u> to Mickey, but he is <u>nervous</u> about revealing his feelings. Actors could communicate this through their use of <u>physical skills</u>.

Physical Skills — Mickey

- Mickey's attraction to Linda is shown by his <u>shy behaviour</u>. An actor could move <u>hesitantly</u> as he "*timidly*" pulls on Linda's <u>wrist</u> and puts his <u>hands</u> on her <u>waist</u>. When she "*beams*" at him, he could <u>break eye contact</u> with her and <u>look away quickly</u> to show how <u>awkward</u> he feels.

- When Linda asks Mickey "what do you care", he could <u>turn his back</u> on her as he says "I don't." — this would suggest he's trying to <u>hide</u> his <u>true feelings</u>.

Physical Skills — Linda

- An actor playing Linda could use <u>helpless body language</u> as she <u>struggles</u> to <u>walk</u> in her high heels — she could stagger and nearly <u>fall over</u> or <u>grab</u> on to Mickey. This would make it seem as though Linda is trying to get Mickey to <u>pay attention</u> to her.

- Linda's <u>confidence</u> could be reflected in her <u>body language</u> — an actor might <u>face</u> Mickey when she speaks to him and <u>lean towards</u> him. When Mickey seems to <u>reject</u> her, she could use a <u>slouched posture</u> and <u>sad facial expression</u> to show her disappointment.

2) A costume designer could choose <u>clothes</u> for Linda that highlight that she is a <u>teenager</u>:

Costume Design — Clothing

- Linda is wearing "*high-heeled shoes*" which suggest she trying to <u>look older</u> than she really is. The shoes might be a <u>bright colour</u> like pink to draw the audience's attention to them and make them seem <u>childish</u>, which would show that Linda is not as <u>mature</u> as she's trying to be. A costume designer might choose <u>broad</u> heels so an actor can <u>move</u> around the stage <u>safely</u>.

- A designer might also put Linda in a <u>school uniform</u> to reflect her <u>youth</u>. Her <u>skirt</u> could be quite <u>short</u> and her <u>tie</u> not <u>fastened</u> properly. This would suggest that she <u>isn't bothered</u> about <u>uniform rules</u>, which would emphasise her <u>rebellious</u> nature.

Act Two — Part One

Mrs Johnstone is reunited with Edward

1) Mrs Johnstone feels a <u>range of emotions</u> in this moment. An actor could convey this using <u>vocal skills</u>.

2) She is <u>taken by surprise</u> when she sees Edward. When she says "Yes, it's, erm... it's in the sideboard...", an actor could <u>stutter</u> and <u>clear her throat</u> during the <u>pauses</u> to suggest that she <u>doesn't know</u> what to <u>say</u>. This would make her sound <u>distracted</u>, as if she can't focus on anything except Edward.

3) The <u>volume</u> of her voice could be <u>low</u> and she could use a <u>gentle tone</u> when she asks "do you still keep that locket I gave y'?" to make her sound <u>warm</u> and <u>affectionate</u>.

4) She overcomes her initial shock and <u>teases</u> Mickey and Edward. An actor could use a <u>slow pace</u> when she says "Oh ... the Essoldo, eh?" and place <u>emphasis</u> on "Essoldo" — this would show that she knows exactly which film they want to see.

Effect on the Audience

Edward could <u>match</u> Mrs Johnstone's <u>quiet volume</u> when he says "Of course". This would highlight that there is still a <u>bond</u> between them.

Set Design — Scenery

- A set designer might make Mrs Johnstone's <u>kitchen</u> look <u>new</u> — everything could be <u>clean</u> and in <u>good condition</u> to suggest that the house has been <u>decorated recently</u>, which would reflect that housing in New Towns was more <u>modern</u> and of <u>better quality</u>.
- The kitchen could be made to look <u>very small</u> — this use of <u>scale</u> would highlight that the Johnstones <u>still can't afford</u> a large house.
- A designer could include <u>wallpaper</u> and <u>curtains</u> to make the kitchen look bright and welcoming. They might have <u>patterned designs</u> in <u>bold colours</u> to reflect the <u>1970s setting</u> of Act Two.

This set uses patterned wallpaper to reflect 1970s styles.

© Donald Cooper/ photostage

Mrs Lyons attacks Mrs Johnstone

1) When Mrs Lyons <u>confronts</u> Mrs Johnstone, the <u>tension gradually builds</u> until a dramatic climax is reached. <u>Music</u> could be used to enhance this for the audience.

2) <u>Incidental cello music</u> could be introduced gradually when the audience sees Mrs Lyons "*appear*". <u>Bass notes</u> and a <u>minor key</u> could be used to create an <u>ominous</u> tone. This <u>non-diegetic</u> music would suggest that Mrs Lyons's intentions are <u>sinister</u>, which would <u>increase</u> the tension on stage.

3) This music could <u>increase</u> in <u>pace</u> and <u>volume</u> until Mrs Johnstone sees Mrs Lyons, then it could <u>cut off</u> abruptly when Mrs Johnstone "*looks up*" — this <u>sudden silence</u> would reflect Mrs Johnstone's "*shock*".

Vocal Skills — Pace and Volume

- Mrs Lyons tries to <u>intimidate</u> Mrs Johnstone — an actor could use a <u>loud volume</u> while she questions Mrs Johnstone to show that Mrs Lyons wants to seem <u>forceful</u>. However, she could also use a <u>fast pace</u> to show that Mrs Lyons is feeling <u>desperate</u>.
- Mrs Johnstone could speak <u>quietly</u> and <u>hesitantly</u> at first to show that she is <u>alarmed</u> by Mrs Lyons appearing in her kitchen. As their interaction goes on, she could use a <u>louder volume</u> and speak more <u>confidently</u> to show that she <u>isn't intimidated</u> by Mrs Lyons. This would show that Mrs Lyons has <u>lost</u> her <u>power</u> over Mrs Johnstone.

EXAM TIP

Got something you're trying to hide? Just locket away...

There isn't a right way or a wrong way to present the play — in the exam, you can get creative about how you'd do it. Just make sure you clearly explain your ideas and the effect they'd have on the audience.

Act Two — Part Two

The second part of Act Two is when everything starts getting really serious for Mickey and Edward. If the audience thinks there's any chance of a happy ending, they really haven't been paying attention...

The second part of Act Two builds towards the tragic ending

1) In Act Two, the <u>pace</u> of the play <u>increases</u> as Russell presents the <u>events</u> leading to the twins' <u>deaths</u>. He shows that their fates are <u>shaped</u> by factors that are out of their <u>control</u>.

© Joan Marcus / ArenaPAL

2) The audience witnesses Mickey, Linda and Edward becoming <u>young adults</u> through a <u>montage</u>. At the same time, the Narrator talks about "<u>changes</u> in the weather" and the "<u>price</u>" the characters will have to pay. The <u>contrast</u> between the teenagers' <u>carefree actions</u> and the Narrator's <u>sinister commentary</u> suggests that their <u>happiness won't last</u>.

3) Mickey's life is <u>happy</u> until he <u>loses his job</u>. This increases the <u>tension</u> for the audience — they can see that his life is being <u>ruined</u> by factors that he has <u>no control</u> over.

4) The play accelerates towards its <u>dramatic ending</u> when Mickey agrees to the <u>robbery</u>. At the same time, Edward confesses his <u>feelings</u> for Linda. These <u>simultaneous</u> moments are <u>frustrating</u> for the audience, as they see both twins making <u>poor choices</u> that will have <u>dangerous consequences</u>.

5) The <u>pace</u> of the action <u>increases</u> even more as Mickey tries to <u>stop</u> taking <u>pills</u>, but then finds out about the <u>affair</u> and goes after Edward with a <u>gun</u>. The audience knows it is <u>too late</u> for him to <u>change</u> his <u>fate</u> and the play moves quickly towards its <u>dramatic conclusion</u>.

The twins age from fifteen to eighteen in a montage

1) Parts of the montage are quite <u>complicated</u> — for example, the Narrator moves between being <u>invisible</u> to the other characters and <u>interacting</u> with them. <u>Lighting</u> can be used to help the audience <u>follow</u> the action on stage:

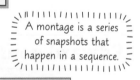
A montage is a series of snapshots that happen in a sequence.

- When the other characters <u>can see</u> the Narrator (e.g. when he takes their photograph at the beach), he could be illuminated by the <u>same spotlight</u> as those characters.
- When he is <u>unseen</u>, he could be lit in a <u>separate pool of light</u> from the other characters.

2) A lighting designer could use a <u>Fresnel</u> focused through a <u>yellow-tinted gel</u> to cast a <u>soft</u>, <u>warm glow</u> on Mickey, Edward and Linda at the rifle range to emphasise their <u>happiness</u>.

3) When the scene "*freezes*", the lighting on these characters could <u>dim</u> and a <u>spotlight</u> could be trained on the Narrator — this would <u>shift</u> the audience's <u>focus</u> on to him and highlight the <u>importance</u> of his words.

4) When the characters are having fun at the <u>beach</u>, <u>gobos</u> could be used to create the impression of <u>waves</u> on the stage to reflect the scene's <u>setting</u>. The tone becomes more <u>ominous</u> as the Narrator talks about "broken bottles in the sand" and "oil in the water" — at this point, the 'waves' could be <u>projected over</u> Mickey, Edward and Linda. This would create a sense of <u>threat</u> and enhance the <u>unsettling atmosphere</u>.

5) When Mickey, Linda and Edward exit the stage and the Narrator is <u>alone</u>, <u>front lighting</u> could be used to cast a large <u>shadow</u> behind the actor. This would make the Narrator seem more <u>menacing</u> and emphasise the <u>sinister</u> nature of his words.

Vocal Skills — Phrasing and Emphasis

- The Narrator's <u>rhyming couplets</u> make it sound like he's telling a <u>sinister nursery rhyme</u>. An actor could use <u>unnatural phrasing</u> and <u>pause</u> between each <u>couplet</u> to enhance this effect.
- As he narrates the montage, he could place <u>emphasis</u> on "fate" and "end" to show that the characters' <u>fates</u> are already sealed.

Act Two — Part Two

Mickey loses his job

1) Russell uses the song 'Miss Jones' to highlight the <u>imbalance</u> of <u>power</u> between <u>working-class</u> and <u>middle-class</u> characters — a set designer could enhance this <u>message</u> through the use of <u>levels</u>.

2) A <u>higher level</u> could be built into the stage design to allow Mr Lyons to be positioned <u>above</u> Mickey and the other <u>working-class</u> characters. This <u>physical distance</u> would act as a <u>visual representation</u> of the <u>class divide</u> for the audience.

3) This level could be accessed by a <u>spiral staircase</u> that's designed so that it can <u>descend</u> into the stage floor. When Miss Jones is <u>fired</u>, she could stand on the <u>top step</u> of the stairs as they are slowly <u>lowered</u> to the <u>lower level</u> where the <u>Dole-ites</u> are positioned. As the stairs disappear into the stage, she would have <u>no way</u> of returning to the <u>higher level</u>. This would reinforce her <u>lack of control</u> over her life to the audience.

© Donald Cooper/ photostage

Physical Skills — Posture

- At the <u>wedding</u>, an actor playing Mickey could use an <u>upright posture</u> to show how <u>happy</u> he is about getting married. His posture could become <u>slouched</u> and <u>subdued</u> when he finds out that he has <u>lost his job</u> — this would show how <u>hopeless</u> he feels once he becomes unemployed.

- The wedding guests who become the Dole-ites could <u>mirror</u> Mickey's <u>posture</u> — this would reinforce that Mickey's situation <u>represents</u> the experiences of many <u>working-class people</u>.

- Mr Lyons could maintain an <u>upright posture</u> throughout this song to show his <u>confidence</u> that his own <u>job</u> is <u>safe</u>. This posture would also emphasise his <u>power</u> and <u>high social status</u>.

Edward confesses to Linda and Mickey agrees to the robbery

1) These two moments have very <u>different moods</u> — <u>interactions</u> between the characters can be used to reinforce this.

2) A <u>tense mood</u> is created when Sammy <u>persuades</u> Mickey to rob the petrol station. An actor playing Sammy might use <u>forceful gestures</u>, <u>unwavering eye contact</u> and <u>put his hand</u> on Mickey's <u>shoulder</u> to make it seem like he is <u>putting pressure</u> on Mickey.

3) An actor might use <u>hesitant body language</u> to show Mickey's <u>uncertainty</u>. He might <u>cross his arms</u> to create a physical barrier between himself and Sammy — this would show that he <u>doesn't trust</u> him and feels <u>intimidated</u> by his behaviour.

4) There is a <u>romantic mood</u> during Edward and Linda's conversation. When Edward says, "if I could be with you", he and Linda could <u>maintain eye contact</u> to show their <u>connection</u>.

Design — Staging

- A <u>large performance space</u> would allow a director to <u>separate</u> the two moments to show that they're taking place in <u>different locations</u>.

- On a <u>thrust stage</u>, Mickey and Sammy could stand on the centre of the <u>apron</u> so the audience can <u>clearly see</u> Mickey's struggle. Edward and Linda could be positioned <u>upstage left</u> so the audience can see their conversation at the <u>same time</u>.

5) They could use <u>tactile movements</u> to show that they are <u>comfortable</u> with each other. For example, Linda could <u>touch</u> Edward on the <u>arm</u> when she says "It's all right", and Edward might <u>take her hand</u> when he says "Then marry me."

Effect on the Audience

While these moments have contrasting tones, both <u>build tension</u> — the audience sees both Edward and Mickey making <u>decisions</u> that may have <u>drastic consequences</u>.

Act Two — Part Two

Mickey finds out about the affair

1) A designer's lighting choices could highlight the contrasting tones in this moment. When the audience sees Mickey *"go to take his pills"*, he could be lit by a dim profile spotlight fitted with a blue gel to create cold lighting. This would signify his dejected state of mind to the audience.

2) In contrast, Edward and Linda could be lit by bright lanterns with pink-tinted gels attached to create a warm atmosphere that reflects their happiness at this moment. The pink light would also symbolise their romantic feelings.

3) A barndoor could be used to block light from part of the stage to create a darker area near the wings so that Mrs Lyons can appear out of the shadows before revealing the affair. This would make her entrance seem foreboding and create a sinister atmosphere.

4) When Mrs Lyons *"points out* Edward *and* Linda" to Mickey, a lighting designer could switch to full lights up — this would symbolise that Mickey knows the truth and the affair is no longer a secret.

5) When Mickey is searching for Edward, spotlights could be used to cast moving beams around the stage to mimic search lights. This would add to the frantic atmosphere in the run up to the play's dramatic climax.

Costume Design — Hair and Make-Up

- A costume designer might make Mrs Lyons appear unkempt and tired — this would show that her worry and fear have taken a toll on her.
- Her hair could be messy and tangled to suggest she hasn't brushed or styled it — this would suggest she has stopped taking care of herself.
- White face powder could be used to make her complexion look pale, while a dark powder could be used to create bags under her eyes. This would make her look ill and tired.

Edward is shot by Mickey

1) When Mickey confronts Edward, an actor could use vocal skills to increase the tension for the audience.

2) An actor could use the pauses in the line "D'y'know who told me about…you…an' Linda…your mother…" to suggest he's still processing the news — he could speak each word carefully as if he can't believe it's true. He could take deep breaths during the pauses to reflect his unstable emotional state.

3) When Mickey shouts "Friends! I could kill you", an actor could suddenly increase the volume of his speech to show that he is starting to lose control. His voice could break when he speaks to show how angry he is and to suggest that he might act impulsively.

4) An actor could use faster breathing and seem to spit out "You! You!" to show his shock and *"rage"*. He could increase the volume and pace of his voice as he says "Why didn't you give me away?" to show his anger is escalating. This would increase the tension for the audience — they know that at some point the twins will die, and Mickey's growing anger makes them wonder if he is going to kill Edward.

© Donald Cooper/ photostage

Sound Design — Sound Effects

- A designer could use recordings of real gunshots to make the guns sound more realistic. This would make this moment feel more frightening and intense for the audience.
- The sound effects could be routed through surround sound speakers to make the audience feel immersed in the action — this would heighten the tension and emotion.

Well, that's quite enough drama for one day...

The play gets quite chaotic towards the end, but your exam answers shouldn't be. Have a clear aim in mind and base the rest of your decisions on achieving that aim — this should keep your answer focused.

Practice Questions

If you thought reading about close analysis was fun, you'll have a cracking time doing some analysis of your own for these practice questions. If you didn't think it was fun... well, have a go at the questions anyway.

Quick Questions

1) What kind of atmosphere might a director try to create when Mrs Johnstone and Mrs Lyons make the pact in Act One?

2) Why might an actor playing Mrs Lyons increase the pace of her speech when she questions Edward about his friendship with Mickey in Act One?

3) What effect would be created if an actor playing Mickey used a high pitch when talking to the Policeman in Act One?

4) Give one way that an actor playing Mickey might use physical skills to show he is reluctant to reveal his feelings for Linda when they walk up the hill in Act Two.

5) How might the set for Mrs Johnstone's kitchen in Act Two reflect the play's context?

6) Why might music in a minor key be played when Mrs Lyons attacks Mrs Johnstone?

7) During the montage in Act Two, how might lighting be used to highlight that the Narrator is a sinister character?

8) How could levels be used to represent the class divide when Mickey loses his job in Act Two?

9) Give one way that an actor playing Mickey might use vocal skills to show his anger when he confronts Edward at the end of the play.

In-depth Questions

1) Describe a costume design for Mrs Johnstone in Act One, then explain how this costume could change in Act Two. Explain the effect of these changes on the audience.

2) What physical skills might an actor playing Mrs Lyons use when Mr Lyons put the shoes on the table in Act One? What would this reveal about her character?

3) How could set design be used to create the 'bus' at the beginning of Act Two?

4) Explain how actors playing Edward and Linda might use vocal skills when he tells her that he's leaving for university. What would this tell the audience about their relationship?

5) Choose a moment from Act Two that involves the Narrator. Explain how a sound designer could use music to create an ominous atmosphere during this moment.

Practice Questions

This is it, the final set of exam-style questions that this book has to offer. Yes, yes, I know you're upset, but still try to spend a good amount of time on each question — you'll be glad you did when exam season rolls around.

Exam-style Questions — AQA

See p.72 for an explanation of how the AQA and OCR exam questions are different.

> Find the part of Act One after Mrs Lyons puts the shoes on the table. Read from where the Narrator says "**There's shoes upon the table an' a joker in the pack.**" to where the Gynaecologist exits, then answer Questions 1 and 2 below.

1) Imagine you're a performer playing the Narrator. Explain how you would use your performance skills to portray him in this extract. You should explain why your ideas are suitable for this extract and for the rest of the play.

2) Imagine you're a set designer working on a production of *Blood Brothers*. Describe how you would use set design to reinforce the action in this part of the play. You should explain why your ideas are suitable for this extract and for the rest of the play.

> Find the part of Act Two where Edward is giving a speech in the town hall. Read from where Edward says "**And if, for once, I agree with Councillor Smith**" to where he says "**No, for God's sake!**" then answer Question 3.

3) Imagine you're a performer playing Edward. Discuss how you would use your vocal and physical skills to portray him in this extract and explain why your ideas are suitable for this extract and for the rest of the play.

Exam-style Questions — OCR

1) Explain how a performer might use vocal skills to portray Mrs Lyons when she moves to Skelmersdale at the end of Act One. Support your answer with examples from the text.

2) Describe how a designer might use stage directions to help them design lighting for the moment after Edward and Mickey come out of the cinema. Use examples from the play to explain why your choices are appropriate.

3) A director is staging the moment in Act Two where Mickey is in prison. How might they direct the performance and the design of this moment to make it engaging for the audience?

About the Exam

This section is crammed full of exam advice and sample answers — what more could you want? Make sure you know whether you're sitting the AQA exam or the OCR exam so you're getting advice for the right course.

'Blood Brothers' will be assessed in a written exam

1) One section of your exam will require you to answer questions on *Blood Brothers*. For this part of the exam, you'll be <u>assessed</u> on your <u>knowledge</u> of <u>how</u> the play could be <u>developed</u> and <u>performed</u>.

2) There will be a <u>mixture</u> of <u>short and longer questions</u>, so it's important that you <u>manage your time</u> carefully — if a question is worth <u>twice the marks</u> of another, you should spend <u>twice as long</u> on it.

If you're sitting the AQA exam, look at the sample answers on p.74-77. If you're sitting the OCR exam, turn to the sample answers on p.78.

3) You'll need to write from <u>different perspectives</u>:

- As a **PERFORMER**, you'll need to think about how you would use your performance skills to portray a certain <u>character</u>. This could include <u>physical skills</u> and <u>vocal skills</u>.

- As a **DESIGNER**, you'll need to come up with <u>design ideas</u> that would enhance the impact of a <u>play</u>. This requires a good <u>understanding</u> of design elements like <u>set</u>, <u>lighting</u> and <u>sound</u>.

4) Some questions might <u>ask</u> about an aspect of design, or you might get to <u>choose</u> which element to focus on, e.g. <u>set</u>, <u>costume</u>, <u>lighting</u> or <u>sound</u>.

The OCR exam will also ask you to write from a director's perspective.

The exams are different for AQA and OCR

The <u>types of questions</u> you'll answer will be <u>different</u> depending on which <u>exam board</u> you're sitting:

AQA

- You'll be asked to write about *Blood Brothers* in <u>Section B</u> of the <u>AQA</u> exam. You'll be given an <u>extract</u> from the play, and you will have to answer <u>four questions</u> about the extract.

- There will be a short-answer question asking you to link <u>design</u> with the play's <u>context</u> or with <u>theatrical conventions</u>.

- Two of the questions will ask about a <u>specific part</u> of the <u>extract</u>.

- The fourth question will require a <u>longer answer</u> that covers the <u>extract as a whole</u>. You can <u>choose</u> whether to answer the question as a <u>performer</u> or a <u>designer</u>.

- All the exam questions for AQA will ask you to refer to <u>the extract</u>, so make sure you've <u>fully understood</u> it before you start writing. <u>Highlight</u> any <u>important words</u> or <u>phrases</u> (including <u>stage directions</u>) and <u>annotate</u> the extract as you <u>read through</u> it. Think about what happens <u>before</u> and <u>after</u> it to help you work out how it <u>fits in</u> with the <u>rest</u> of the play.

- Some questions will also ask you to write about <u>the play as a whole</u>, so you'll need to <u>relate your ideas</u> about how to stage the extract to other <u>ideas</u> or <u>events</u> in the play.

OCR

- You'll be asked to write about *Blood Brothers* in <u>Section A</u> of the <u>OCR</u> exam. There will be <u>eight questions</u> and you'll have to <u>choose</u> the *Blood Brothers* <u>option</u> each time.

- The questions will cover different aspects of staging *Blood Brothers* including <u>performance</u>, <u>design</u> and <u>directing</u>, and you'll need to write about the play's <u>context</u>.

- There'll be a <u>variety</u> of <u>question styles</u>. You may be asked about <u>specific parts</u> of the text or given <u>visual prompts</u> like <u>photos</u>. You might have to write your answer in <u>different ways</u>, e.g. in a <u>table</u>.

- As well as writing from the perspective of a <u>performer</u> and a <u>designer</u>, you'll need to answer as a <u>director</u>. This involves writing about how a director would bring a <u>written text</u> to life <u>on stage</u>, including <u>decisions</u> you would make about aspects of <u>design</u> and <u>performance</u> in the play.

- You will be asked to <u>support</u> your answers using <u>examples</u> from the play.

About the Exam

There are some things you'll always need to do in the exam

1) No matter which exam board you're using, there are <u>certain aspects</u> that you'll need to consider:

- Russell's <u>intentions</u> and what he wants to convey — <u>stage directions</u> are useful for this.
- how the play's <u>historical</u>, <u>social</u>, <u>cultural</u> and <u>theatrical contexts</u> might <u>affect</u> a production.
- the <u>roles</u> and <u>responsibilities</u> of <u>theatre makers</u> and how they bring the play to life, as well as any <u>challenges</u> they may face.
- how the <u>genres</u> and <u>style</u> of the play can be <u>conveyed</u> to the <u>audience</u>.

2) Use accurate <u>technical language</u> when describing aspects of <u>performance skills</u>, <u>design features</u> and <u>stage configurations</u>.

3) Use <u>examples</u> (e.g. <u>quotes</u>, <u>context</u> or <u>events</u>) that demonstrate <u>understanding</u> of the play and <u>support</u> the point you're making.

4) Give <u>specific</u>, <u>detailed</u> suggestions on <u>how</u> you'd <u>perform</u>, <u>design</u> or <u>direct</u> a production to help the examiner <u>visualise</u> your ideas.

5) Describe the <u>desired effect</u> of a production on the <u>audience</u>, as well as <u>how</u> this effect might be <u>created</u> using <u>theatrical techniques</u>.

> For AQA, you can include drawings in your answers to help the examiner picture your ideas (you can also do this for OCR if the question says you can). You won't be judged on the quality of your drawings, but your work should be legible.

Shorter answers should be concise

You shouldn't spend lots of time on <u>short-answer</u> questions that aren't worth many marks. Your <u>answers</u> should be <u>snappy</u> and <u>straight to the point</u>. Have a look at this example:

> Imagine you are a set designer for a production of *Blood Brothers*. Suggest a set design for the Lyonses' house at the start of Act One and explain why your choices are appropriate. You should refer to the play's context in your answer.

The first sentence <u>addresses</u> the question.

Act One is set in the mid-20th century and the Lyonses are a wealthy middle-class family, so I'd make the set design for their house seem realistic for that setting and context. I would cover flats in wallpaper to create the interior walls of the house. The wallpaper would feature delicate purple flowers and green leaves to reflect the 1950s and 1960s fashions of patterned materials and bright colours. I would hang framed landscape paintings on the walls and paint the frames gold to create a sense of "opulence". I would construct the "table" out of an expensive wood, like mahogany, that is highly polished. This would show that it is high quality and emphasise that the Lyonses are wealthy.

The explanations are <u>brief</u> and <u>relate closely</u> to the question.

The sentences are generally <u>short</u> with <u>clear points</u>.

Manage your time carefully in the exam...

The questions will be worth different marks. Make sure that you don't spend too much time on questions that are worth fewer marks — plan ahead so you know roughly how long you should spend on each one.

AQA Sample Answer — Performance

If you're sitting the AQA exam, these are the pages for you. For the long question, you can write about either performance or design, so we've done a sample answer on each. If you're doing the OCR exam, skip to p.78.

Here's a sample question about performance

Here's what a long question about performance might look like:

> Read Act Two, from where Edward says "**What about the job you had?**" to where Edward "***slowly backs away***", then answer the question below.
>
> You are part of a production of *Blood Brothers*.
> Imagine you are a performer who is playing the role of Edward. Discuss how you would use your performance skills to portray Edward in this extract. You should explain why your ideas are appropriate for this extract, and for the rest of the play.

The extract will be printed in full in your exam — read the extract carefully and annotate it with your initial thoughts and ideas.

Here's how you could plan your answer...

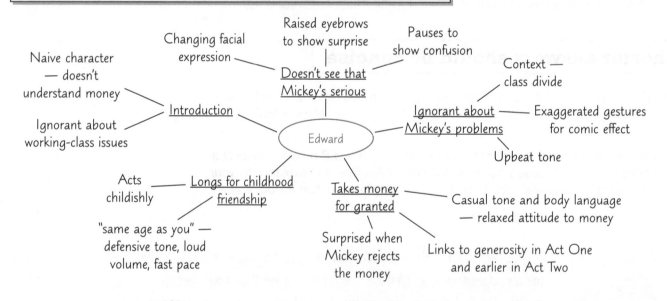

... and here's how you could write it

Keep your introduction brief and focused on the question.

Edward is a very naive character — he has had a privileged life and doesn't understand the importance of money. This is clearly shown when Mickey tells Edward that he is unemployed. In this extract, an actor would need to use their performance skills to communicate Edward's ignorance about the difficulties faced by the working class to the audience.

At the beginning of the extract, I would choose to show that it takes Edward a while to realise how serious Mickey's situation is. I would use a cheerful facial expression at the start of the extract, then I would gradually make my expression more serious as Mickey is speaking to suggest that Edward is slowly realising how

This picks out one aspect of the character and explains how it might be performed.

AQA Sample Answer — Performance

upset Mickey is. I would raise my eyebrows when Mickey says "I bleedin' hated that job" to show Edward's surprise at the harshness of what Mickey is saying. I would pause in between "Why... why" and ask the question slowly. This would reinforce that Edward is confused by what Mickey has said and is still processing the information.

> Use short quotes to make it clear to the examiner which part of the extract you're referring to.

In this extract, Edward has an idealised view of unemployment. I would use his reaction to Mickey's confession to emphasise this. I would use a light and upbeat tone when Edward says "If I couldn't get a job I'd ... tilt my hat to the world" and accompany this with an over-the-top gesture where I would mime tilting a hat. This would show that Edward is trying to be funny, which would highlight that he still hasn't fully grasped the seriousness of their conversation. This portrayal would make Edward seem flippant and show that he doesn't understand the realities of living in poverty, which would reflect that middle-class people like Edward weren't as badly affected as working-class people like Mickey during the recession in the 1970s.

> Make a range of points about vocal and physical skills.

> This shows that you've considered the play's context.

In this extract, Edward tries to solve Mickey's problems by giving him money because he doesn't fully understand Mickey's situation. The stage directions say that Edward tries to "throw some notes" to Mickey. I would eagerly reach into my pockets when I say "Look, look, money" and pull out the notes to show that Edward is keen to give Mickey money and expects him to accept it. Elsewhere in the play, I would have used a casual tone and body language when he gives him sweets in Act One and offers to get him cigarettes earlier in Act Two to show that Edward is happy to be generous towards Mickey. In this extract, I would use the same casual behaviour to show that he doesn't think that giving money is any different from giving sweets or cigarettes. I would recoil in shock when Mickey throws the notes on the floor. This body language would show that Edward wasn't expecting Mickey's reaction. I would pick the notes up quickly and clumsily to show that Edward is flustered, emphasising his confusion to the audience.

> This shows good awareness of the play as a whole.

> Explain how your choices are either similar or different to the rest of the play.

> Always explain the effect of your performance decisions.

At the end of the extract, I would want to reveal Edward's desire for the simplicity of childhood friendship. I would put stress on the words "blood brothers" to highlight this meaningful phrase for the audience, and I would use a respectful tone to show Edward places a lot of value on their childhood pact. As I say that line, I would step towards Mickey. This close proximity would signal Edward's desire for friendship. I would use a defensive tone for "I'm exactly the same age as you", speaking quickly and loudly and placing emphasis on "you". This would make it sound like a childish retort to Mickey's "you still are a kid", showing the audience that he isn't as mature as Mickey. Edward realises that their relationship has changed, but he still doesn't understand why. Before he leaves, he "looks at Mickey". I would stare at him with a hard facial expression that slowly softens into a hurt one before breaking eye contact to convey feelings of defeat and hurt.

> This considers the impact of the portrayal on the audience.

> You can quote stage directions, but you should add your own ideas to them.

I can't go to the theatre — I get terrible stage fright...

You'll need to explain your answers in more detail in these longer questions, but all your points should be relevant to the question. Don't get off track and start raving about how the Milkman's the best character...

AQA Sample Answer — Design

We've got another lovely AQA sample answer for you — this time it's all about design. Whether you're a budding set designer or you think *Blood Brothers* would be better with a few added puppets, read on...

Here's a sample question about design

Here's what a <u>long question</u> about <u>design</u> might look like:

> Read Act Two, from where Edward says "**What about the job you had?**" to where Edward "***slowly backs away***", then answer the question below.
>
> You are part of a production of *Blood Brothers*.
> Imagine you are a designer working on this extract of the play. Explain how you would use design skills to reinforce the action in this extract for the audience. You should explain why your ideas are appropriate for this extract, and for the rest of the play.

> You can choose the aspect of design you want to focus on — set, lighting, sound, costume or puppet design. Pick the one you feel confident writing about. The sample answer below focuses on costume design.

Here's how you could plan your answer...

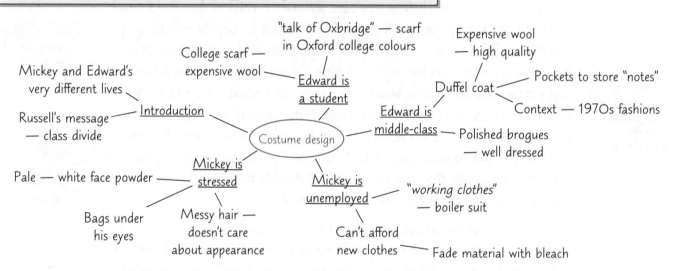

"talk of Oxbridge" — scarf in Oxford college colours

Expensive wool — high quality

College scarf — expensive wool

Edward is a student

Mickey and Edward's very different lives

Russell's message — class divide

Introduction

Duffel coat

Pockets to store "notes"

Context — 1970s fashions

Costume design

Edward is middle-class

Polished brogues — well dressed

Pale — white face powder

Mickey is stressed

Mickey is unemployed

"working clothes" — boiler suit

Bags under his eyes

Messy hair — doesn't care about appearance

Can't afford new clothes

Fade material with bleach

... and here's how you could write it

When staging this extract, I would use costume design to convey the difference in Mickey and Edward's wealth, class and lifestyles. This would highlight Russell's message about the difference in the opportunities that are available to the twins as a result of their social class.

> This describes the <u>overall effect</u> you want to achieve.

This extract takes place at Christmas when Edward has just come back from university. The stage directions state that he is wearing a "*college scarf*". This is a symbol of his new university lifestyle and highlights his status as a privileged student so I would use it to emphasise his wealth and educational advantages. I would choose a scarf made of expensive cashmere to show it is high quality. Earlier in Act Two, Edward's

> You can use <u>stage directions</u> from the play to support your ideas.

AQA Sample Answer — Design

This shows good awareness of the play as a whole.

teacher says there is "Talk of Oxbridge" in Edward's future, so I would use the official colours of Oxford University's Corpus Christi college for the scarf. This would signify that he is a member of an elite group who have access to a good education.

I would use the rest of Edward's clothing to reinforce his wealth and middle-class status. The stage directions state that he is wearing a "*duffel coat*", so I would choose a tan-coloured coat with a hood and toggles to reflect 1970s fashions. The coat would be made from an expensive material like wool to suggest that it is high quality, and it would be in good condition to show that it is new. I would dress him in well-fitting, tailored trousers to suggest that he has had them specially made. This would show the audience that Edward can afford to buy expensive new clothes. The stage directions state that Edward "*tries to throw some notes*" to Mickey, so his coat would need to have pockets to store the "notes". I would sew additional pockets onto the inside of the coat so he could pull money from several places, and I would make sure that the pockets were easy to access so they wouldn't hinder the actor's performance. For his shoes, I would choose a pair of polished brogues to add to his well-dressed appearance and make him look formal.

This shows that you've considered the play's context.

This shows that the answer considers the whole extract.

The answer looks at how design supports the action of the extract.

In this extract, Mickey has been made redundant and is struggling to find work, but he's still wearing the "*working clothes*" that he wore during 'Miss Jones' before the start of the extract. Mickey worked in a box factory, so I would dress him in a dark blue, polyester boiler suit to reflect the uniform that a factory worker might have worn in the 1970s. I would spray the boiler suit with a mixture of bleach and water to fade the material to make it look worn. This would suggest that it was already old when Mickey got it, showing that, unlike Edward, he can't afford new clothes. For Mickey's shoes, I would choose steel-capped boots to reflect 1970s work shoes. I would distress the leather on the boots using a brush with metal bristles to make the boots looked scuffed, showing that they are in poor condition. The contrast between these shoes and Edward's smart brogues would be an effective representation of the class divide for the audience and enhance the impact of Mickey's words when he says "But I'm not in your shoes, I'm in these".

This shows good knowledge of the rest of the play.

This provides specific detail about the techniques that you'd use.

This considers the impact of the portrayal on the audience.

Explain the reasons behind your design choices.

I would ruffle up Mickey's hair to make him look unkempt and suggest that he is too stressed to care about his appearance. In contrast, Edward's hair would be combed into a neat side-parting to emphasise that he has time to take care of himself and is not stressed like Mickey. I would also use make-up to make Mickey look tired. I would apply white face powder to make him look pale and use a darker powder under his eyes to suggest he hasn't been sleeping well. This would show the impact that searching for jobs has had on him and would also make him look older than Edward. This would reinforce the effect of Mickey's words for the audience when he says that Edward is "still a kid" whereas he "grew up".

You can use quotes from the play to explain the effect of your ideas

---

There are no mistakes in my plays — it's all by design...

For the 20-mark design question, it's important to give lots of detail when explaining your ideas, so be specific about the design choices you'd make, and describe what you'd do to achieve the right effect.

OCR Sample Answers

OCR students, this is the page for you. In the exam, you'll have to tackle short questions about performance, design, directing — all sorts. Have a read of these sample answers and we'll show you how it can be done...

You may be asked about a specific line in the play

In Act One, Mrs Johnstone says "**With one more baby we could have managed.**" Explore the effect that this line has on Mrs Johnstone in *Blood Brothers*.

This gives a <u>specific example</u> of how the line affects her later in the play.

Mrs Johnstone knows she can afford to raise one more child but not two. This destroys her hope that her job with the Lyonses will end her struggle to support her large family. This makes her feel desperate and vulnerable, so it is easier for Mrs Lyons to manipulate her into giving Edward away. This results in her separation from Edward for most of his life, and leads to the tragic deaths of both of her sons when she reveals that she gave one of them away.

This explains the <u>impact</u> of the line on Mrs Johnstone.

Here's a sample question about directing

A director is staging the final scene of *Blood Brothers*, when Mickey shoots Edward. Explore how they might direct the performers to make this scene engaging for the audience.

In the exam, you can choose to write about the direction of performers, the direction of design, or both of these.

This shows you understand the <u>role</u> of a director.

The director could position Mickey and Edward at opposite sides of the stage to create distance between the brothers. This lack of proximity would show how far they have been driven apart, visually highlighting their fractured relationship for the audience. The director could position Mrs Johnstone in between the twins, standing slightly closer to Mickey to show that her focus is on him. Linda could be positioned upstage at a distance from Mickey, Edward and Mrs Johnstone. This would create tension for the audience as they wait to see if she will intervene. It is Mrs Johnstone who acts — when she walks "*slowly*" towards her sons, a director could direct her to use slow and gentle movements to suggest she doesn't want to alarm Mickey. This would encourage the audience to be wary of how Mickey might react. The director might tell Mickey to use quick and erratic movements to show his state of distress. This would heighten the tension of this scene for the audience — they know that the situation will escalate and result in the twins' deaths, but they aren't sure how or when. The director might instruct Edward to stand still and quiet, his attention focused on Mickey — this would reflect that what happens is out of his control.

You should use <u>examples</u> from the play to <u>support</u> your ideas.

Explain how your choices would <u>engage</u> the <u>audience</u>.

EXAM TIP

Lights, camera — wait, wrong type of director...

These questions in the OCR exam only require short answers, but there'll be lots of them, so you can't afford to spend too much time on each one. Make sure you get straight to the point in your answers.

Glossary

antagonist	A character who causes trouble for the protagonist.
apron	A part of a stage that extends beyond the curtain.
backdrop	A large cloth that is hung at the back of the stage. It often has scenery painted on it.
backstory	The events that have happened to a character before the action of the play.
barndoor	A metal flap that can be attached to a stage lantern and used to shape its light beam.
birdie	A small stage lantern which casts a bright, soft-edged beam of light.
black box theatre	A small theatre with a black interior. The seating can be rearranged to suit the performance.
body language	The way movements, posture and gestures can show how someone feels without speaking.
Brecht, Bertolt	A German theatre maker who played a major role in the development of epic theatre.
catharsis	The sense of release felt by an audience when a play makes them feel strong emotions.
characterisation	The way an actor interprets and performs their character.
choreography	A rehearsed sequence of steps or movements.
composite set	A set which shows multiple locations on stage at the same time.
convention	A feature of staging, design or performance that is associated with a particular style or time.
cross-cutting	When two or more scenes which take place at different times or in different places are performed on stage at the same time.
cyclical structure	A plot structure which starts and finishes at the same point in the narrative.
cyclorama	A curved screen at the back of the stage which can have scenery projected onto it.
dialogue	The general term for any lines spoken between characters.
diegetic sound	A sound that can be heard by the characters in a play.
downlighting	When the stage is lit from above to highlight certain characters or cast shadows.
dramatic irony	When the audience knows something that the characters don't.
end-on stage	A proscenium arch stage without the arch to frame it.
epic theatre	A style of theatre made famous by Bertolt Brecht. It tries to distance the audience from the action of the play so that they can concentrate on the overall message.
flat	A wooden frame with canvas stretched over it which is painted and used as scenery.
floodlight	A type of stage lantern which casts a broad wash of light onto the stage.
flying rig	A piece of equipment that the actors or scenery can be suspended from.
foreshadowing	When a playwright hints at something that is going to happen later in the play.
form	The type of written drama (e.g. play, opera, musical, pantomime).
fourth wall	The imaginary barrier that separates the audience from the world of the play on stage.
Fresnel spotlight	A type of stage lantern which casts a beam with a softly defined edge.
gauze screen	A cloth screen that can appear transparent or opaque depending on how it is lit.

Glossary

gel	A piece of <u>coloured</u>, <u>heat-resistant</u>, <u>plastic film</u> used to <u>change</u> the <u>colour</u> of a lantern's <u>beam</u>.
genre	The <u>type of story</u> a play is telling (e.g. <u>comedy</u>, <u>tragedy</u>).
gesture	A <u>movement</u> made by <u>part of the body</u> (e.g. arms, head) to convey a character's <u>emotions</u>.
gobo	A <u>thin</u>, <u>metal disc</u> with <u>shapes</u> cut into it which can be slotted into a lantern to <u>project patterns</u> or <u>images</u> onto the <u>stage</u> or a <u>backdrop</u>.
improvisation	When drama is <u>made up</u> on the spot by performers <u>without</u> using any <u>prepared material</u>.
incidental music	Any <u>music</u> which <u>accompanies</u> a performance and is used to create <u>mood</u> or <u>tension</u>.
inflection	Changes in the <u>pitch</u> and <u>tone</u> of a person's <u>voice</u> as they speak.
intonation	The <u>rise</u> and <u>fall</u> of a performer's <u>voice</u> to create a <u>natural</u> pattern of speech.
lighting rig	A <u>structure</u> above the stage and wings which <u>holds</u> the <u>stage lanterns</u>.
line of sight	The <u>audience's view</u> of the <u>action</u> on <u>stage</u>.
linear structure	A plot structure where the events on stage happen in <u>chronological order</u>.
mannerism	A <u>repeated</u> physical or vocal <u>habit</u> that contributes to <u>characterisation</u>.
minimalist set	A <u>basic set</u> that uses <u>minimal</u> scenery and <u>very few</u> props.
minor character	A character who isn't important to the plot but <u>adds depth</u> to the world of the play.
montage	A <u>series</u> of <u>short scenes</u> that show <u>snapshots</u> of time in a <u>sequence</u>.
mood	The <u>atmosphere</u> at a particular <u>moment</u> that creates a <u>feeling</u> or <u>emotion</u> for the audience.
musical	A type of play that uses <u>song</u> and <u>dance</u> to <u>develop the plot</u> and <u>entertain the audience.</u>
narrator	A character who <u>comments</u> on the action and the plot to the <u>audience</u>. A narrator can be <u>first-person</u> (involved in the action) or <u>third-person</u> (set apart from the action).
naturalism	A style of theatre which tries to recreate <u>real life</u> on stage <u>as closely as possible</u>. In contrast, a <u>non-naturalistic</u> style includes features that <u>remind</u> the audience what they're watching <u>isn't real</u>.
New Town	Towns that were <u>redeveloped</u> after the Second World War to provide <u>more housing</u>.
non-diegetic sound	A sound that <u>can't be heard</u> by the <u>characters</u> in the play.
phrasing	The way a character's <u>dialogue</u> is <u>broken up</u> into <u>sections</u> when spoken by an actor.
pitch	How <u>high</u> or <u>low</u> an actor's <u>voice</u> is.
plot	The <u>series of events</u> that takes place in a play.
posture	The <u>position</u> a character holds themselves in when <u>sitting</u> or <u>standing</u>.
production note	Russell's <u>notes</u> at the start of the play that give <u>suggestions</u> about <u>how</u> the play should be <u>staged</u>.
profile spotlight	A type of stage lantern that produces a <u>sharply defined beam</u>. These lanterns are used to <u>focus</u> on a <u>particular character</u> or <u>part of the stage</u>.
promenade theatre	A style of theatre that requires the audience to <u>follow</u> the actors between <u>different performance spaces</u> over the course of the play. This usually takes place <u>outdoors</u>.
prop	An item on stage that the characters can <u>interact</u> with. If a prop is <u>specific</u> to <u>one character</u>, it's called a <u>personal prop</u>.

Glossary

Glossary

proscenium arch stage	A box-shaped stage which is set back from the audience so that only the front end is open to them, framed by the proscenium arch itself.
protagonist	The main character in a story.
proxemics	The use of the physical space between the actors on stage to create meaning.
pyrotechnics	A theatrical firework display which is used to create dramatic effects on stage.
Received Pronunciation	An accent that is considered the accent of Standard English in the UK and has the highest social status.
recession	A period of economic decline where business activity slows down and people earn and spend less money.
reverb	An effect that can be applied to a recorded sound to make it echo.
revolving stage	A stage or part of a stage which can spin around.
rostrum (plural rostra)	A raised platform which is used to introduce different levels to the stage.
silhouette	A dark outline of the performers or scenery which is created using a backlight.
site-specific theatre	A style of staging which temporarily transforms somewhere that isn't a theatre into a performance space. This space often resembles the play's setting in some way.
soundscape	A collection of individual sounds that are layered up to create a strong sense of place.
stage directions	Any instructions written in a script by the playwright to explain how a play should be performed.
stage furniture	Any moveable object on stage which isn't a costume, a prop or a part of the scenery.
stereotype	An oversimplified idea about what a person is like that is based on a group they belong to.
straight play	A non-musical play that uses dialogue to tell its story, rather than music or dance.
stress	In vocal performance, the emphasis a performer places on certain words and phrases.
strobe	A type of stage lantern which rapidly flashes on and off.
structure	The shape of a play's narrative, including the order in which it's shown to the audience.
style	The way in which a director chooses to interpret a performance text on stage.
symbolism	The use of props, gestures, setting, lighting, etc. to represent other things and create meaning.
Theatre in Education	A movement that encourages the use of theatre to enhance education in schools.
theatre in the round	A style of staging which seats the audience on all sides of a central stage.
thrust stage	A stage which extends out into the audience, so that they're standing or sitting on three sides.
tragedy	A genre of play which features a serious plot and an unhappy ending.
traverse stage	A long, narrow stage which runs between the audience, who face the stage on both sides.
truck	A structure on wheels which can be painted on both sides and used as scenery.
underscoring	Incidental music that is played quietly during a scene under spoken dialogue or visual action.
uplighting	When the stage is lit from below to create an unusual or unsettling effect.
wings	The space to the side of a stage which is used for storage and as a waiting area for the actors.

Index

Phew! After all that, you should know *Blood Brothers* like the back of your hand. But if you'd like a quick recap of the play's plot (and maybe even a chuckle or two), read through *Blood Brothers — The Cartoon...*

Mrs Johnstone

Mickey Johnstone

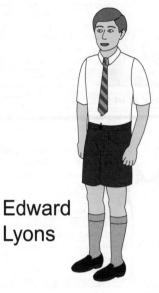

Edward Lyons

Mrs Lyons

Mr Lyons

Sammy Johnstone

Linda

Narrator

Willy Russell's 'Blood Brothers'